Praise for *What's Up wit*

Govan and Smith trace stages of ident
serve in white women as we come to re .... .ocations in
sexist systems that oppress us and racial systems which privilege us.
The book is alive with white women's testimonies on the raw but rewarding work of observing often hidden power systems. This analysis helps white women with two simultaneous character-forming
tasks: healing from wounds of sexism and using the power we get
from privilege to weaken racism in ourselves and in the world.

— Peggy McIntosh, PhD, author, *White Privilege:
Unpacking the Invisible Knapsack*,
founder, National SEED Project on Inclusive Curriculum,
Wellesley Centers for Women

Bold, poignant, and provocative, Govan and Smith have done a mas-
terful job of highlighting vital voices, frameworks, and analysis of
white women and racism that is rare. This work is much needed in
this time of racial reckoning. This is a must read for those looking to
go deep to understand how complicity, niceness, and silence can be
equally as devastating as racism itself. Thank you!

— Tyrone C. Howard, PhD, professor,
UCLA Dept of Education and Black Male Institute

Combining a joint approach for addressing sexism, in partnership
with the privilege of whiteness, along with the proposed identity development model and concrete actions, this book promises to move
the work of anti-racist white women forward by leaps and bounds.
If you identify as white and female and are serious about your anti-
racism work in the world, this is your next book.

— Kathy Obear, Center for Transformation and Change,
author, *But I'm NOT Racist* and *In It For The Long Haul*

Is there a need for a book on white women and racial justice work?
Having read this book, the answer is clearly yes. Govan and Smith
have struck a powerful balance which allows this book to at once
speak truth, offer hope, and expect the reader to act. The experience
of both authors' ever-deepening work in this area shines through
and is a valuable model for how white women can engage in racial
justice practice.

— Dr. Heather W. Hackman, president, Hackman Consulting Group

White women are both bulwarks in maintaining white supremacy and leaders of resistance to it. This book is an insightful, provocative, and practical guide to the range of ways white women respond to the intersection of gender and race. With nuance, and attention to complexity, Govan and Smith do an excellent job of teasing apart the many roles that white women play in our communities and offer them a challenge to examine the complicated impact of gender and race in their lives. Filled with poignant, powerful, and honest stories, this book offers a toolkit for white women to become more effective racial justice allies. Highly recommended.

— Paul Kivel, educator, activist, author,
Uprooting Racism: How White People Can Work for Racial Justice

I always appreciate it when white women tell other white women about being white women. This book does not disappoint. Reading through the developmental process leading from Immersion to Integration, I saw decades of my interactions with white women finally making sense! The stories, histories, examples, and experiences that Govan and Smith provide are both personal, painful, and enlightening. This book offers a timely opportunity for white women to learn more about themselves as they work toward the Integration of their race and gender intersections.

— Dr. Debra Ren-Etta Sullivan, Seattle Black Child Development Institute

Govan and Smith have created an excellent resource to help white women better understand their conflicting position as victims of sexism and as perpetrators of white supremacy and racism. The book offers new ways of thinking and tools to enable white women to overcome lack of information, fear, and resistance, which will better prepare them to work to dismantle systems of oppression. I salute the authors for having the wisdom and courage to write this valuable book.

— Pamela Smith Chambers, training director,
The Beyond Diversity Resource Center,
co-author, *The Anti-Racist Cookbook*

What's Up with White Women? is a turning point in our collective understanding of a group that exercises racial privilege but is trapped by sexism. The authors deftly walk readers through an understanding of white women with bravery and empathy rarely seen in books on anti-oppression.

— Robin Parker, executive director, Beyond Diversity Resource Center,
co-author, *The Anti-Racist Cookbook*

WHAT'S UP
WITH WHITE
WOMEN?

WHAT'S UP
with WHITE
WOMEN?

**UNPACKING SEXISM AND WHITE PRIVILEGE
IN PURSUIT OF RACIAL JUSTICE**

ILSA GOVAN AND TILMAN SMITH

new society
PUBLISHERS

Cover design by Diane McIntosh. ©iStock

Printed in Canada. First printing September, 2021.

Inquiries regarding requests to reprint all or part of *What's Up with White Women?*
should be addressed to New Society Publishers at the address below.
To order directly from the publishers, please call toll-free (North America)
1-800-567-6772, or order online at www.newsociety.com

Any other inquiries can be directed by mail to:

New Society Publishers
P.O. Box 189, Gabriola Island, BC V0R 1X0, Canada
(250) 247-9737

LIBRARY AND ARCHIVES CANADA CATALOGUING IN PUBLICATION

Title: What's up with white women? : unpacking sexism and white privilege
in pursuit of racial justice / Ilsa Govan and Tilman Smith.

Names: Govan, Ilsa M., author. | Smith, Tilman, author.

Description: Includes bibliographical references and index.

Identifiers: Canadiana (print) 20210264640 | Canadiana (ebook) 20210264667 |
ISBN 9780865719613 (softcover) | ISBN 9781550927542 (PDF) |
ISBN 9781771423502 (EPUB)

Subjects: LCSH: Anti-racism. | LCSH: Women, White—Attitudes. | LCSH: Women,
White—Social conditions. | LCSH: Privilege (Social psychology) | LCSH: Racism—
Social aspects. | LCSH: Racism—Psychological aspects. | LCSH: Race relations. |
LCSH: Race awareness. | LCSH: Sex discrimination against women.

Classification: LCC HT1521 .G68 2021 | DDC 305.8—dc23

 Canadä

Funded by the Government of Canada
Financé par le gouvernement du Canada

New Society Publishers' mission is to publish books that contribute
in fundamental ways to building an ecologically sustainable and just society,
and to do so with the least possible impact on the environment,
in a manner that models this vision.

 new society
PUBLISHERS

Certified
B Corporation

MIX
Paper from responsible sources
FSC
www.fsc.org
FSC® C016245

This book is an offering to our white sisters
in solidarity and with love.

It is dedicated to all of the People of Color
who have asked us to take an honest look
at ourselves and collect our people.

Contents

Foreword

by Shakti Butler

In 1955, when I was 8 years old, the violent murder of 14 year old Emmet Till turned my world upside down. Carolyn Bryant, a white female, generated the lie resulting in a young person's brutal murder. The 21-year-old woman testified in court that Emmett had grabbed and verbally harassed her in a grocery store. "I was just scared to death," she said. The all-white jury cleared her husband Roy Bryant and his half-brother JW Milam of the crime. They later publicly admitted their guilt, saying they wanted to "warn other coloreds." At 62 years of age, Carolyn admitted that she had fabricated her testimony.

What's Up with White Women? presents a detailed model for re-framing oppression stemming from internalized supremacy and sexism. Emotional behaviors, attitudes, and practices—whether rationalized or invisibilized—stem from colonialized hierarchies of power. White women must be willing and able to explore and address these internalized beliefs and actions that perpetuate white supremacist patterns, inflaming continued emotional and physical violence. This invaluable book highlights strategic rationalized behaviors—both unconscious and conscious. Govan and Smith provide an invitation for white women to look more closely at the complicated and ongoing dynamics that perpetuate inequity, violence, and deep separation from having authentic relationships internally, externally, and structurally with people of color.

It is Friday evening. This is to be a weekend with Resmaa Menakem and the opening presentation is being offered to Black, Indigenous, and People of Color (BIPOC). We line up in groups of four and historical truths are whispered into the ear of each person standing at the beginning of the line. The four people represent a four generational passage of time. No words are spoken to anyone else and soon the atmosphere in the room is thick—saturated with pain and suffering... the result of genocide, rape, torture, enslavement, forced removal, and cultural impalement. Tears, groans, and moans are expressed by almost everyone. Bodily impact is physical and emotional. This is intergenerational trauma passed along from one to the next.

Two days later the white women participate in a similar process. The narrative is from the vantage point of the oppressor. The woman at the front of each line is told a story. An 8-year-old child is at the park. It's a beautiful day and many people—adults and children—are gathered. A lynching is the focal point of attention. The response to the pinnacle of dehumanization is met with confused and "deadly" dissociation.

Addressing behaviors that emanate from deeply ruptured connections to racialization and adherence to sexism—as illustrated by the cold response I witnessed in the white women during Resmaa's workshop—lies at the core of this book. The emotional and intellectual postures are actually strategies that are attempts to sublimate any responsibility or accountability for being a part of keeping the invisible from being visible. The model of identity development the authors present is interlaced with narrative examples; the voices and lived experiences of the authors and many others. The results are clear and accessible examples of predictable rationalizations that help sustain behaviors, attitudes, and assumptions that have been deeply driven into U.S. societal rules, regulations, and cultural ways of being.

The narrative examples incorporate the sea change required to address anti-oppression development. Clearly, oppression does not produce societal well-being internally or externally. Ancestral and contemporary trauma impacts people's lives, relationships, lack of fair access to opportunities, all of which are encoded in U.S. history through laws, practices, structures, and culture. It literally and figuratively forces people into "positions" that disrupt collective well-being. It undermines safety, trust and loving relationships. Colonization and the culture of supremacy continually replicates rampant individualism, disconnection, and dehumanization.

When Tilman and Ilsa invited me to write the foreword for this critical work, my curiosity prompted me to ask them why they wanted a Black, mixed-race woman to join them in this printed space; a space so clearly aimed at deconstructing white women's racial privilege and gender marginalization. Addressing this question was personally important. Having been in relationship with the authors, both professionally and personally, I could trust the diligence and commitment that stands behind their internal explorations, as well as their research of many years. And yet, I have to admit, I felt a certain degree of caution given the ways that women of color are used to advance agendas that have reproduced the systemic wheel driving racialized outcomes. For these reasons, their request begged a clarifying response regarding their motivation. Yes, inviting me, a woman of color, to pen this forward was intentional on their part and my acceptance of their request rested upon whether or not there could be agreement regarding the validity of their ideas related to human development. To that question, I emphatically agree that what is being offered to the reader, particularly those who are willing to courageously inquire into the sticky layers of oppression, is pure gold!

What's Up with White Women? extends critical human-centered tools and approaches for confronting deep dilemmas in contemporary society. We must resist the structural erosion of civil and human rights. What is so generously offered in this meticulous body of work is clarity, authenticity, truth telling, and active participation in healing practices. What is being offered is substantive guidance towards building a more informed and liberated public.

SHAKTI BUTLER, PhD is a dynamic filmmaker and visionary educator in the field of racial justice and liberation. She is the Founder & President of World Trust Educational Services, an organization she established over two decades ago. Through films, dialogues, and Learning Labs, World Trust addresses pertinent social issues related to healing, radical imagination, and liberation.

Acknowledgments

MG, you are a dear friend and co-conspirator. Thank you for the belly laughs, deep talks over dinner and walks, and off-hand insights that changed our lives. We love you.

This book would not exist without our core focus group participants, Katy, Mallory, Chris, Johanna, and Terrie, who fleshed out ideas and taught us what we were missing. As we read your words, we continue to smile, cry, and feel inspired.

We deeply appreciate the generosity of focus group participants at the White Privilege Conference: Peggy, Christine, Ilana, Beth A., Laura, Shelly, Robin, Beth Y., Dena, and Jessica. Your stories and lives enrich the world.

Thank you to Darlene for transcribing everyone's words so carefully. You are missed.

As we developed the model, we brought it to Women of Color doing anti-oppression work and asked for their feedback and insights. Dr. Caprice D. Hollins, Elsie Dennis, Inez Torres Davis, Shakti Butler, Stephanie Puentes, Anita Garcia Morales, and Toi Sing Woo all contributed their thinking. Thank you all for your valuable contributions. We also brought the model and content to Peggy McIntosh, who supported us unfalteringly from that first meeting. Her insights, critique, and encouragement buoyed us throughout our process. We love and appreciate you, Peggy.

Fran Davidson, Denise Michaels, Mayet Dalila, Wei Li Chen, and Toi Sing Woo helped develop the institutional analysis. We owe huge gratitude to all the ways they've informed our thinking.

Theressa Lenear has supported us at every step of our process, by helping to develop the institutional analysis, providing feedback on the developmental model, and, finally, by providing critical and loving feedback on our manuscript. We thank you for your tireless generosity, brilliant mind, and revolutionary love.

We're indebted to Dr. Eddie Moore, Jr. and The Privilege Institute for providing a place for us to practice our skills, mess up, hold workshops, try out our ideas, and network with other amazing social justice activists across the US.

We thought a lot about the cover of this book and are deeply grateful to Roger Shimomura for inspiring us all the way. Your grace and patience with our requests will never be forgotten. Thank you.

For your willingness to review our manuscript and give invaluable guidance, we thank Karena Hooks, Tami Farber, Evangeline Weiss, and Diana Falchuk. We especially want to thank Rachel Chapman, whose critical feedback throughout the book shone a light on all we had missed and all we still have to learn. The book is better because of all of you.

Thank you to all of the wonderful people at New Society Publishers who helped us actualize this text we've labored over for the past six years into a published manuscript. We are grateful to be able to work with a publisher whose values of social and environmental justice align with ours.

This text was written by authors who occupy the land of the Duwamish and Coast Salish people. Thank you for stewarding this land for generations.

Ilsa

Over the past thirteen years, the countless conversations I've had with my wonderful business partner, Dr. Caprice D. Hollins, have shaped my thinking about white privilege in more ways than I can name. Many of the ideas in this text came from our conversations and from watching you facilitate. You're the first person I call for comfort and to help me better understand when everything goes sideways in a workshop. Thank you, my friend.

Sophie Bjork James, our conversation in the bar at the White

Privilege Conference (WPC) was pivotal in my reexamination of sexism.

Paul Ruiz, I love you. I so appreciate the support to go on writing retreats or even just being able to say, "I need to shut my office door today." Thank you for giving me the space to write and the backyard cocktail hours around the fire pit.

Thank you to my mom, dad, sister, and brother-in-law for helping me explore different ways of navigating patriarchy and white privilege throughout my life. Jenn, you've seen me through many of these stages, and your unwavering friendship has made me a better person. My awesome crew of girlfriends, Dawn, Penny, Jasmine, and Brenna, make me laugh and support me through the roughest of times.

Wentworth P. Merryweather, you make me smile every day. You're a good boy.

I'd also like to recognize the semicolon. Without this tool, my dear friend Tilman would be lost. Tilman—I love you and all of the time we've grown together and pooled our creative energy, especially in the ocean.

Tilman

There are not enough words to express my love for my life partner, husband, and best friend Michael. Thank you for never faltering and always believing. Thank you for being honest about white men.

Brady and Langston, I cannot imagine life without you. Your presence makes me a better person and saved me from a life of sadness. Thank you for being such wonderful and beautiful people, men, and sons.

For Supremia Elizabeth Coley, for deliberately and carefully teaching me that there was another way. Without romanticizing our relationship, I thank you for saving my life. And for your family who were forced to live without their mother, grandmother, sister, and friend.

What would I do without you, Ann O'Donoghue? From the moment we met, my life got better. You are the best friend a person could ever have.

Thank you to Cultures Connecting for supporting this work from the very beginning. Especially to Caprice, for your kindness, genius, and grace.

Our profound thanks goes to Shakti Butler, for elevating our hearts and minds with your revolutionary vision, generosity, and luminous work, and for your brilliant foreword. We love you.

I also lovingly give thanks to Sandria Woods Pollard, Debra Sullivan, Sharon Cronin, Mayet Dalila, Toi Sing Woo, Annie Erickson, Christy Erickson, Bernie Alonzo, Andrea Rabinowitz, Francine Seders, Mako Nakagawa, Janet Davidson Hues, Bif Brigman, Dale Watanabe, Taylor Cassell, Delbert Richardson, Donald Felder, the Wingo Family, the Remington Moore Family, Heather Hackman, Carrie Gibson, Pamela Chambers, Robin Parker, Paul Kivel, Vicki Sween, Rick Butler, Antonia Darder, Cam Do Wong, Zakiya Stewart, Jocelyn Myers, Barbara Daniels, Kim Francisco, Katie Graham, Larry Matsuda, LueRachelle Brim-Atkins, the Matschke Family, BCDI Seattle, The People's Institute of Survival and Beyond, my Wedgwood neighbors, CCR Colleagues, and the Pacific Oaks College NW Family.

Ilsa, thank you for every single moment we have spent together figuring this out. I am a better person for having you in my life. I love you.

1

Introduction

No one ever talks about the moment you found out that you were White. Or the moment you found out you were Black. That's a profound revelation. The minute you find that out, something happens. You have to renegotiate everything.

— Toni Morrison

A FEW YEARS AGO, we were invited to be a part of the planning team supporting a national anti-racism conference in the Seattle area. We felt honored to be the only two white women selected by a Black man to serve on the local executive leadership committee. We love this conference, and the fact that we were chosen for this important role said a lot in our minds about how awesome we are and how different (and let's be honest, how much better) we are than other white people.

This started out as a collaboration run by a multiracial team and ended up with us micromanaging and trying to take control of every aspect of the planning process. With little provocation, we convinced one another that we had to take over for the "good of the conference." After all, if we didn't oversee and double-check each committee's work, send out all of the emails, plan the agendas for our meetings, and call the conference organizer whenever we felt we needed to, who would?

While we understood how to follow the leadership of Black people in theory, when it came to our actual practice, we actively exhibited the white supremacy behaviors described by Kenneth Jones and Tema Okun in their article *White Supremacy Culture,* such as hoarding information, creating a sense of urgency, believing there is only one right way (the white way), thinking we were the only ones who knew the right way, and feeling a right to our comfort. At the same time, we opportunistically held onto the dichotomous idea that we were good people and, therefore, we couldn't possibly be oppressive.

This left many of the People of Color (PoC) we were supposed to be partnering with shaking their heads in frustration and saying, "What's up with white women?!" Although, to be honest, they already knew the answer.

Despite the fact that we joined the committee with years of experience in anti-racism work, we still resisted hearing any critical feedback from our colleagues during the planning of the conference. With time, we became more self-reflective, self-aware, open, and honest about our assumptions and behaviors on this team. Our hope in writing this book is to help both ourselves and other white women identify our racism more quickly, receive critical feedback more openly, and recover and make amends more graciously.

We write this book as a love letter to our white sisters. We hope it will help you recognize how we can engage in our everyday lives, work, and activism more effectively, and ultimately contribute, in many small ways, to our collective liberation. We hope it will help you sleep easier, knowing your actions are better aligned with how you see yourself and the core values that guide you. After all, the movement for social justice needs us to be brave, wide awake, and well-rested.

We also write this book as an offering to the People of Color who love, live with, work with, or simply have to interact with white women. Should you choose to read further, we hope this book will name and help explain some of the patterns you've witnessed in white women. We understand and own the harm that we inflict upon you regularly and humbly invite you to read these pages, not as a rationale for our behaviors, but as a window into our individual and collective journeys toward liberation.

We are at a particular moment in the United States when the

need for white women to understand and effectively navigate multicultural partnerships has become a regular part of the public discourse. We've seen countless news stories of white women threatening Black lives by calling the police on Black people for anything from telling them to leash their dogs, to selling water, to sitting in a Starbucks. In the 2020 election, white women recently provided an even larger base of support for Donald Trump than in 2016. We have also shown up in large numbers at Black Lives Matter protests and worked to mobilize our siblings across the country to oppose racist violence.

At the same time as we're seeing heightened awareness of racism, we are experiencing a public reckoning with sexism as witnessed in the Women's March, #MeToo, and the upsurge in intersectional feminism. In all of these instances, white women have both hindered and helped to advance social justice.

This book explores the ways in which white women in the United States are positioned in a hierarchy between white men and People of Color, a buffer zone, due to our racial privilege and gender marginalization. We'll examine how we internalize beliefs about our own inferiority due to sexism and, at the same time, internalize our racial superiority. Using theory, history, and true stories shared in focus groups, we highlight patterns in white women's behaviors used to survive sexism in a patriarchal society and strategies we've developed to get ahead despite barriers. We'll explore how these same patterns have been used to sabotage People of Color, resulting in deep conflicts and pain, as we prioritize our access to privilege. The heart of this book is a model of identity development where we name six distinct phases to explain the different ways white women navigate both sexism and white privilege: Immersion, Capitulation, Defense, Projection, Balance, and Integration.

The Canyon We Must Cross

Imagine standing on the edge of a canyon. Our internalized sexism and white superiority tell us to hold our ground and stay "safe." This false sense of safety is a mindset that exploits people and the planet and will ultimately lead to physical, spiritual, and psychological destruction that actually makes us far less safe. On the other side of the canyon are our core values of justice, love, authentic relationships, and shared wisdom, to name a few. On that other side exists collective liberation—a concept we can easily say but not so easily envision—where we recognize the deep interconnection necessary to our survival as a species. The gap between feels like a frightening space. It is a space of practicing new ways of being and often failing in this practice. A space where we risk losing friendships and family who prefer the false comfort and dehumanization of racist systems designed to serve white people.

The canyon between our actions and beliefs can manifest like this: I value equity and relationship, but when I disagree with a Person of Color, I do so in a way that intentionally re-centers my white privilege in lieu of equity. For instance, a Chinese American man points out that our new policy might exclude communities who don't speak English. Instead of asking questions for more understanding, I defend my decision and may reiterate that there is a time crunch, or that there are "rules" that need to be followed. While I may cloak my assertions in kindness and high regard for him and for all of the communities we serve (how I want to see myself), there is no doubt my arguments are meant to remind this man that I know more and better understand how systems work (how I am actually behaving).

White women stand on the edge of that canyon and decide whether we're willing to leap across or stay put. We feel the allure of staying where we are and the stronger pull to live in a place aligned with our core values. In making the jump, we realize the canyon isn't nearly as wide, or scary, or dangerous. It is merely a small crack in the earth. This book is a product of our experiences of trying to recognize and jump over those cracks, of understanding what keeps us frozen on one side and learning how to take an uncertain leap toward liberation. The beauty of our friendship and alliance as the authors of this work is that it allows us the option of holding hands and leaping over together.

Working in Relationship

The authors, who are both white women, first met over fifteen years ago when Tilman's younger son was in Ilsa's fifth-grade class. We remember this time differently. For Tilman, Ilsa provided a safe haven for her child while she worried about retaliation because of her activism in the school. Ilsa was in her third year of teaching fifth grade, still overwhelmed by, well, everything, and just happy to have a parent supporting her social and environmental justice agenda. We both saw something in the other that drew us together.

Our friendship and deep love for one another grew over time, as we worked separately and collaboratively as racial equity consultants and community activists. We partnered for many years in an anti-racist educator's organization we co-created with other white women called WEACT, The Work of European Americans as Cultural Teachers. Tilman has seen Ilsa through the start and growth of her business, Cultures Connecting, with Dr. Caprice Hollins. Ilsa has seen Tilman through her work for racial justice in early childhood education as a coach, educator, and manager in nonprofits and government agencies.

Our relationship is based on a shared passion for uprooting systems of oppression, coupled with a fair amount of self-deprecating humor. We hold each other as mentors, asking ourselves in critical moments, "What would 'Tilsan' do?" We remind one another of the mantra we created together with our friend MG: "Stop, Take a Breath (STAB)", where we engage in the healthy processing of reactivity and anger in our bodies.

By working together, we intentionally counter the sexist and racist competition so common among white women. Instead, we refer to ourselves as "accountabilibuddies," holding up a mirror for one another in our efforts to counter systems of oppression.

As two white women learning and practicing together, we sometimes notice a gap between our core values and our actions, as evidenced by our experience planning the conference. Ilsa remembers sharing a long, self-righteous email she'd written to a Black woman in reaction to what she saw as an uninformed critique in one of her workshops. Tilman lovingly responded that, no matter what the critique was from the Black woman, Ilsa's multiple links to articles and attempts to prove herself more knowledgeable than this woman weren't the best cross-cultural practice and were probably rooted in anti-Blackness. Gulp. Now I'll enjoy a slice of this humble pie and do something entirely different next time.

At one point when we were working on our book, Ilsa gently pointed out to Tilman, "You seem to have a lot of white women you don't get along with." Hmmm. Yep, I'll be thinking about that for years to come.

This book would not have existed without our third Circle Belle (our band name if we had a band), MG Lentz. They helped co-create the identity development model that is the foundation of this book. Though they chose not to co-author the book, they helped create the framework and continue to inform our thinking.

From our conversations with MG, we developed a workshop for white women to gather and explore the unique intersection of our identities. What started in the spring of 2012 as a one-day session looking at the model we'd created quickly shifted to a two-day intensive with deep self-awareness work around how the interlocking experiences of sexism and white privilege have harmed us, and how we've harmed others. We collectively grew our knowledge of where white women are positioned in the United States in our ability to access institutional power. And we shared new skills and strategies to improve our relationships with People of Color and one another and address institutional oppression. The wisdom shared in these workshops by hundreds of women over the years greatly informs the content of this book. Many of the women who first met in these workshops have also stayed connected, continuing to grow and advocate for change together.

A Push

There is also no way we could have written this book without the insights from Women of Color. Inez Torres Davis, a Mujerista-Indigenous woman, wrote us,

So often white women use their own victimization as a wild card to get them out of the mess, an almost-free pass that means they don't have near as much work to do around their privilege as white men have! I refuse to allow you to be ignorant of the blood that marks the places where white women scrape from themselves their need to do their own work. That smear, that blood contains both of our DNA.

My suffering at the hands of white women runs deep. White women push me out of their way expecting me to see their shove as a push in a better direction.

We listened. And we examined the behaviors white women display that are not only irritating but harmful to People of Color. At first, we wanted to excuse ourselves from this group of white women who cause the suffering Inez named, to see ourselves as the exception to the rule. The idea that we were oppressive was especially challenging to see in ourselves because we understood through personal experience the damage of oppression that sexism has on our lives. Then we felt confused because as good people doing good things, how was it possible we didn't have insights into the ways we were harming others? We had internalized that our push *was* in a better direction.

Instead of stopping with a defensive posture, assuming we were different, or granting ourselves "good one" status, we became curious about what we were missing. What is this chasm that is so hard for us to acknowledge and so obvious to Women of Color?

Along with thousands of others, we benefited from the wisdom of our mentor, Dr. Peggy McIntosh, whose seminal work, *White Privilege: Unpacking the Invisible Knapsack*, provided that moment Toni Morrison names when we realized we were white and had to renegotiate everything. Dr. McIntosh's insight, "After I realized the extent to which men work from a base of unacknowledged privilege, I understood that much of their oppressiveness was unconscious. Then I remembered the frequent charges from Women of Color that white women whom they encounter are oppressive. I began to understand why we are justly seen as oppressive, even when we don't see ourselves that way," launched us into an investigation of how we can both experience sexism and internalize a sense of superiority. Dr. McIntosh also helped us to see that our oppressive beliefs and behaviors have everything to do with history and socialization, and very little to do with whether or not we are good people.

At the same time as we recognized we were missing pieces of the puzzle related to our privilege, we noticed that any conversation about sexism in racial justice circles was immediately shut down as trying to wiggle out of responsibility. We were getting the message loud and clear, "Do not equate your experiences with sexism with racial oppression," with which we whole-heartedly agree with and readily avoid. While we do share some gender issues, racism creates vast chasms in how sexism plays out in the lives of Women of Color compared to white women.

However, having to check our experiences with sexism at the door also felt like we were missing a piece. We wanted a way to talk about both sexism and racism that didn't rely on comparison or competition. How were we carrying the pain of sexism with us, in our minds and bodies, and how was this informed by our white privilege? How was our whiteness informing our experiences with patriarchy? We began conversations with other white women about what it would mean to examine sexism alongside, rather than instead of, internalized white superiority.

Focus Groups

White privilege allows white women to ignore or minimize racial dynamics most of the time, and many avoid conversations about race and racism. Because of our work as anti-racist organizers and consultants, we have had the unique opportunity to regularly witness, and often facilitate, explicit conversations about racism and white privilege. This means we see and hear white women talk about race in our everyday lives far more often than most white people do. In creating the identity development model, we drew extensively from our experiences in workshops to illuminate white women's patterns when we engage in race conversations.

To further develop our understanding of the model we were creating, not depend solely on People of Color to educate us, and better illustrate what we saw as each stage of identity development, we formed a focus group of white women in Seattle that included Mallory Clarke, Johanna Eager, Katy Greenleaf, Chris Schafer, and Terrie Yaffe. We met monthly for two hours over six months. This group was intentionally composed of women of different ages, sexual orientations, religions, and class backgrounds. Some had attended our workshops, and all had been involved in anti-racism work through their jobs, relationships, and community activism.

We also asked white women who attended the White Privilege Conference, a national anti-racism conference founded by a Black man, Dr. Eddie Moore, Jr., to form two focus groups at the 2014 event. Each of these groups was composed of diverse white women who had been involved in anti-racism scholarship and activism across the country for years. The participants were Beth Applegate, Robin DiAngelo, Ilana Marcucci-Morris, Peggy McIntosh, Laura Moore, Dena Samuels, Christine Saxman, Shelly Tochluk, and Beth Yohe. These groups each met for two hours to discuss how they saw race and gender intersecting in their lives.

When we formed the focus groups, we imagined the participants' stories would give life to the model. Instead, we found listening to and rereading their experiences and insights made the book far more of a collaborative project. Many times, they spoke to an idea we had never considered, and an entire subsection of the book emerged as a result. As we describe the stages of the model, we have embedded their stories. They are the heart of our work, and we are deeply grateful for the risks they took in opening up with us.

Throughout the book, we refer to each of these women by their first name unless they requested to be anonymous (except for the two Beths, because writing Beth O. and Beth A. feels too much like elementary school). You can read a little more about each of their backgrounds and identities in the appendix, and you probably should because they are all awesome.

The Power of Language

We thought a lot about what pronouns to use for white women throughout the book. We landed on using "we" (occasionally "she" or "her") when referring to any person who identifies as a white woman. This is to be clear we are including ourselves, the authors, in all of the phases and behaviors we describe. This does not mean *all* white women demonstrate *all* the patterns we identify. We invite white women readers to notice when you have a strong reaction to being seen as part of the "we." We also do not assume all readers of the book identify as white or women, and we're glad you're choosing to join us in our exploration.

It is our hope this text will be accessible to as many people as possible. We know people can mean different things with the same words, which can get confusing and sometimes obstruct understanding. We have unpacked terminology as we use it throughout the text. You can also find our operating definitions of sexism, internalized oppression, internalized superiority, racism, white privilege, and other important concepts in the appendix.

Acknowledging Our Lens

We recognize that factors beyond race and gender also shaped the way we approached and interpreted white women's experiences and want to be transparent in the lenses we bring. Tilman's Norwegian and English ancestry influences her value of stoicism, her sense of scarcity, her tendency to compartmentalize emotions, and her genuine fondness for slapstick humor. Ilsa's German, Polish, French, and Romanian ethnicity, as well as growing up in the Midwest, informs her sense of timeliness, her taste for sarcasm, and her desire to avoid conflict but willingly gossip. The authors are both cisgender, US born, and not experiencing disabilities. Tilman comes from an upper-class background and Ilsa from a working-class background. Tilman is heterosexual and Ilsa is queer, and both are in long-term relationships with cisgender white men. Tilman is spiritual and Ilsa an atheist, and both come from Christian-based families. Tilman is the mother of two sons, and Ilsa is the mother of Wentworth P. Merryweather, a very good dog.

No model of identity development will capture every person's experiences, and we did not attempt to create a comprehensive guide for all white women. Our focus groups did not include white trans* or gender-nonconforming women, and we don't assume they experience all aspects of internalized sexism in the same way as white cis women. Nor do we have stories from white women living in extreme poverty or those with disabilities, who may experience white privilege and sexism differently. At the same time, we believe all white women will likely see some reflection of themselves in the phases of the model we developed. People of Color and white men may also identify with some of the behaviors we've highlighted. Rather than limiting the conversation to only those who see this model as a full-length mirror of their experience, it is instead our intention to create a window to deepen and broaden future work.

2

A Power Analysis:
White Women
and Institutional Access

THE ECONOMIC SYSTEM and driver of policy in the United States is capitalism, and this particular system that values capital, wealth, and accumulated assets, was created by and for white men via colonization, genocide, and slavery. Wealthy white men's historic exploitation of people and the environment put them in the position to create institutions that protect the capitalist system and their related interests to this day. Every institution in the US, both formal and informal, including health care, government, criminal justice, education, banking, and many others, is run on policies, structures, time, and resources designed to maintain white male power.

One need only do this simple exercise created by Dr. Joy DeGruy to recognize this truth.[1] List white-controlled institutions in the US and the negative impacts they have on Communities of Color. Next list People of Color-controlled institutions and the negative impact of these on white communities. It is likely your first list includes life-changing outcomes such as poor education, mass incarceration, and even death, while the second list consists primarily of individual exclusions or discomfort, such as not being able to attend an Historically Black College or University (HBCU) or not having some businesses you go into cater to you (such as a barber or restaurant). This provides a simple illustration of why "reverse racism" doesn't exist when we understand racism in the context of institutional benefits rather than individ-ual discrimination.

We base our definition of racism on that of the legacy of ac-tivists from the People's Institute for Survival and Beyond: "In-stitutional Power + Prejudice against subordinated members of targeted racial groups (Blacks, Latinx, Native Americans, Asians) by members of the agent racial group (whites). This happens at the individual, cultural, and institutional level. Racism can in-volve both conscious action and unconscious collusion. In other words, it need not be intentional."

Given that US institutions were created by white men to serve the needs of white men, it makes sense that white men more easily and inequitably access these systems. They were literally built to do so.

Why is access to institutions important? This has meant being able to build wealth off of the exploitation of unpaid or under-paid individuals, owning land taken from the Indigenous inhab-itants, and getting 95 percent of Veteran's Administration home loans after WWII (just a few of many examples). The ease with which people can access institutions in this country determines daily experiences, including how you are educated, how you are protected or not protected, where you get to live, where you get your food, if you have potable water to drink and use, and what kind of medical services you do or don't receive. For those of us who have relatively easy access, many of these things can be taken for granted. But for people who do not have easy—or any—access, life is proportionately more difficult and dangerous.

Navigating Sexism

Sexism creates barriers to accessing institutional power for women. National statistics show that violence against cisgender women is a genuine threat to our daily lives, with an even higher risk for trans* and gender nonconforming women. For example, in the National Center for Transgender Equality's 2015 US Trans-gender Survey, almost one in ten Black respondents had been physically attacked for being transgender in the past year, with the compounding factors of both racism and transphobia.[2]

Sexism can also lead to lower pay and/or lack of access to employment, health care, childcare, and education. The recent #MeToo movement, founded by an African American woman, Tarana Burke, has cracked open the door of our collective understanding of how men, and predominantly white men, have created barriers to institutional access for women by using sexist tactics. While sexual harassment is being illuminated in the United States more in recent years with the Women's March and #MeToo campaign, most women have always known that sexism is real. Therefore, women must have strategies to survive individual acts of sexism, systems that thrive off of our underpaid or unpaid labor, and our disproportionate lack of access to resources to get through our lives.

When we don't recognize that sexism comes in the form of institutional barriers, women are more likely to believe they, and other women, are personally to blame for any mistreatment or lack of progress they make. Women applying principles of male dominance and oppression to themselves and/or other women is called internalized oppression. The People's Institute of Survival and Beyond defines internalized oppression as "a multigenerational, disempowering, dehumanizing process that creates dependency [in this case on white men]. It manifests itself as rage/fear, shame, denial, self-hatred, worthlessness, self-destruction, exaggerated visibility, and exaggerated invisibility. It eats away at one's humanity and sense of well-being, and comes in the form of adaptation, distancing, assimilation, colorism, tolerance, protectionism and mimicry, and instant gratification."[3] Any group or individual experiencing oppression can demonstrate the internalization of their oppression to different degrees at different times. Throughout the book, we'll further explore the dynamics of white women's internalized sexism in regard to ourselves and how we see and treat other women.

Benefiting from White Privilege

While sexism is integral to white women's experiences, so is whiteness. The idea that "white is right" can permeate our interactions and our assumptions about ourselves, leading to internalized superiority in our beliefs and actions toward People of Color. In other words, we may come to believe that our socially and politically superior status as white people is normal and deserved.

White women as a whole have more intimate access to white men. They are our fathers, brothers, uncles, and sons. Much of our access to power is dependent on how well we can work with or around white men. Our strategies, both conscious and unconscious, in relationship to white men include paying extra attention when they are speaking, asking a question rather than giving a direction, deferring to white men even when we think they are wrong, backing off from our arguments if we sense they are getting irritated or angry, laughing at their jokes, and crying when we feel misunderstood, helpless, or afraid of what is to come. These strategies are important to our safety and advancement, whether we are cognizant of using them or not. They can be effective ways to deal with the concrete reality of interpersonal, cultural, and institutional gender discrimination and violence.

Many white women can relate to using these relationships to get our everyday needs met. When Tilman needed a car, she knew that she would receive better service and ultimately a better price if her husband Michael bought it. To do this, she and Michael found a car online, and Michael went to buy it alone. He returned in a short time with the car and a good price.

In the study "Race and Gender Discrimination in Bargaining for a New Car," which examined negotiations for more than 300 new cars, it was found that Chicago car dealers offered Black and female testers significantly higher prices than the white males with whom they were paired, even though all testers used identical bargaining strategies.[4] A 2015 study in the *New York Times Economic Review* showed that Black people pay an average of $662 more than white people when buying cars.[5] So, it makes good economic sense for white women to rely on white men in our lives to purchase automobiles.

Another way white women benefit from proximity to white men is that we learn how to behave in ways to help us gain power and control in the workplace. We have emulated and internalized the lessons on white male cultural norms, values, and behaviors that help us navigate institutions. Some of these norms include prioritizing hierarchy, timeliness over relationships, strict control of and limited access to information, and either/or thinking. If we've used these tools to successfully navigate sexism and gain controlling positions in our jobs, we may feel simultaneously entitled to sustain this control and concerned about losing it.

This explains why white women in organizations with a mission statement focused on racial justice may be able to "talk the talk" but are unwilling to give up any of the benefits of whiteness and "walk the walk" of said mission. Some resulting behaviors can include micromanaging people's work activities and communication, taking over meetings with rigid and intense speech and expectations, creating a sense of urgency that doesn't allow for multiple perspectives, and interjecting our opinions and synopses even when not asked for or needed. We may make performative gestures toward racial justice and signal to others how different we are from other white people (who are obviously the problem) without doing anything to challenge the status quo of the workplace, especially if this would mean risking our jobs.

While white women can gain power through our relationships with white men, we also pay a price for this power. In 1988, Deniz Kandiyoti coined the term *patriarchal bargain* in her article "Bargaining with Patriarchy."[6] The term refers to a woman's decision to conform to the demands of patriarchy to gain some benefit, whether it is financial, physical, psychological, emotional, or social. The trade-off for us is that we often abdicate our inherent power, rights to sovereignty, and intelligence to cash in on the presumption of protection and ease. It leads us to believe that men have our backs when this is not often true. As Jaime Phlegar wrote, "One problem with patriarchal bargains is that they pressure women into internalizing patriarchal ideologies and, thus, either knowingly or unknowingly recreating patriarchy every day. Even if some of these bargains are 'easy' for women to make—even if they do not bring immediate harm to women's own lives or if they make an individual woman's life easier in the short term—it reinforces a system of oppression for all women. There is an individual gain, but a collective loss."[7]

It is important to understand that not all white women want or have close relationships with white men who provide this transactional pathway. This may be influenced by class, religion, immigrant status, disability, age, sexual orientation, or other areas of personal identity. For example, straight women of all races can leverage sexual attraction with white men, resulting in different levels of access to privilege and power. They may also be less likely to risk challenging a straight white man than queer women because they've internalized the value of not endangering potential partnerships. (This is true whether either party is currently in a relationship.)

Occupying the Buffer Zone

White women's position in the hierarchy of institutional access lies between white men and People of Color. We are the nurses, teachers, realtors, office managers, nonprofit staff, and nonprofit directors. This creates a dynamic that encourages and rewards white women to act as enforcers of policies and practices for white men and institutions. In other words, white men make the rules and white women make sure everyone follows the rules. One simple example of this is a pattern we've noticed while teaching adults over the past twenty years. White women are the population most likely to ask questions about instructions on an assignment. Asking, "Are we doing this right?" is usually followed by Helpful Holly explaining the instructions again to everyone in her group.

A more damaging trend of enforcement is how white women middle managers in nonprofits control the flow of information and materials to People of Color and poor people while insisting they are following the regulations set out by funding institutions. We've witnessed many executive directors who won't stand up for racial justice if it means upsetting donors or board members.

Paul Kivel refers to this position as the "buffer zone." He says,

"People in the ruling class—those who are the top of the economic pyramid—have never wanted to deal directly with people on the bottom of the pyramid but have wanted to prevent them from organizing for power. Therefore, they have created a space that protects them from the rest of the population. I call this space the *buffer zone*."[8]

For example, in the book *Impossible Subjects: Illegal Aliens and the Making of Modern America*, Mae Ngai points out how wealthy white men used the myth of Filipino men taking jobs and then dating white women to justify violence in the late 1920s and '30s. Ngai writes, "Thus anti-Filipino hostility was a site where ideas about gender, sexuality, class, and colonialism intersected in violent ways and, moreover, informed the construction of the racial identity of both European and Filipino migrants. That process gave immigrant workers from southern and eastern Europe a purchase on whiteness, which was part of their own Americanization. By contrast, Filipinos were denied their American acculturation and reclassified into an identity that combined racial representations of Negroes and Orientals."[9]

In many ways, this narrative blamed white women when poor white men attacked Filipino men. This was a continuation of othering rooted in the myth of the Black man as rapist. It is one example of how American racial identity has been intentionally constructed and how the "need to protect white women" has been used to justify racist violence.

Throughout US history, those in the ruling class have utilized tactics of division among those with less institutional access to maintain their position at the top. The concept of the buffer zone helps us better understand how white women protect and insulate white male power, even at our own expense.

White women have relatively less power than white men and relatively greater visibility and proximity to People of Color through our jobs in helping professions. Therefore, it can be easier to identify and villainize individual white women than it is white men. Think about the popular narrative of people who call

911 on Black people: BBQ Becky, Golfcart Gail, Permit Patty, and Cornerstore Carolyne to name a few. Do white women call 911 more than white men?

White men are more likely to just take matters into their own hands rather than needing systemic backing, as was the case when they hunted and murdered Trayvon Martin and Ahmaud Arbery. When white women call the police on Black people, we are using the weaponized institution of white patriarchy to threaten Black lives. The "Karen" trope is sexist only if we don't realize that she is using white male-controlled systems to wield her power. We need to ask ourselves why we feel entitled to control the actions of People of Color and how it is connected to our position in the buffer zone.

Mamta Motwani Accapadi points out the obstacles to holding white women accountable for their racist actions: "While white women are members of an oppressed group based on gender, they still experience privilege based on race. This dual oppressor/ oppressed identity often becomes a root of tension when white women are challenged to consider their white privilege by Women of Color."[10] If and when we are challenged about the aforementioned behaviors, we often feign innocence or ignorance and claim to be misunderstood. We might circle back with other white women to gossip about the Woman of Color and ultimately have her expelled from the organization or group. These moments of feeling misunderstood are frequently coupled with tears and/or retribution, thus maintaining our position of power in the hierarchy just below white men.

Any analysis of our white privilege that disregards sexism is incomplete. For example, our friends and activists Evangeline Weiss and Kari Points facilitate workshops for white women that start with the story of Carolyn Bryant and Emmett Till. On her deathbed, Bryant admitted Till never whistled or made any comments to her. However, she was not the one who originally accused him. Her husband's brother was in the store and called Roy Bryant with this story. Living with an abusive husband, Carolyn decided to collude with white supremacy, which ultimately led to the brutal murder of Till.

This does not excuse Bryant of responsibility; it complicates the common narrative that focuses more on Carolyn's accusation and rarely mentions that this also came from her brother-in-law. As such, the story as it is typically recounted deflects attention from the underlying issue of white male privilege and the often-violent maintenance of systems of oppression. Again, there are multiple cases in history where sexism and the so-called protection of a white woman were used to justify white men killing Black men and other Men of Color. Yet, even in our activist work for racial justice, we have witnessed white women in the buffer zone receive more critical feedback around our racism than the white men on top.

The dynamic of division and competition to get to the top is key here. The white woman who plays the best enforcer while capitulating to white male egos ends up ahead, at least temporarily. This creates a tension between white women that helps to keep sexism in place, simultaneously disconnects us from People of Color, and, thus, insidiously prevents us from unifying to collectively change this dehumanizing and environmentally destructive hierarchy.

White women can both help and hinder movements for justice in the United States. The model of identity development we created highlights how, as we progress in our self-awareness and knowledge of institutional white supremacy, white women can strive to learn from our past oppressive actions and illuminate creative, mutually liberating ways of being in partnerships across the hierarchical divides.

3

A Model of
White Women's Development

*If you open the smallest toolbox, you will find only one tool,
a hammer…Opening the second box, we find it also has a
hammer in it. But it has another tool as well, say a wire-cutter.
With this toolbox we can do more—we can cut wire, as well as
pound things. Each skill set provides us with more "tools," more
skills, and more possible courses of action. The final skill set is
the ultimate toolbox; it has every possible tool in every possible
size. This ultimate toolbox also provides assistance, handing
us the tool we need at the moment we need it…[The] simpler
and more conditioned skills take less energy to use, and we are
more practiced with them, so we tend to default to them. These
fundamental skills don't foster liberation or even knowledge
of oppression. Instead, they are part of the mechanism for
maintaining the status quo. They are easy to use and habitual.*

— Leticia Nieto

ETHNIC AND RACIAL IDENTITY development models by
Drs. William E. Cross, Jr., Donald R. Atkinson, George Morten, Sanra K. Bennett, Beverly Daniel Tatum, Janet Helms, Leticia Nieto, and others have contributed greatly to our understanding of how we interact cross-culturally, how we perceive our own race, and how we address and respond to institutional racism. They document different stages as people navigate dynamics of

FIGURE 3.1. Intersections of Sexism and White Supremacy in White Women's Anti-Oppression Development

HEGEMONY ↔ LIBERATION

Immersion	Capitulation	Defense	Projection	Balance	Integration
Racism/ Internalized White Supremacy Willful • Internalized Sexism Active	Racism/ Internalized White Supremacy Passive • Awareness of Internalized & Institutional Sexism	Awakened Awareness of Racism/ White Supremacy • Heightened/ Hyper Awareness & Defensiveness about Sexism	Heightened/ Hyper Awareness of Individual & Institutional Racism/ White Supremacy • Denial of Importance of Internalized Sexism	Understands Anti-Racism/ Internalized White Supremacy • Understands Individual, Internalized & Institutional Sexism	Actualization of Integral Connection Between Anti-Racist Practice and Liberation from Sexism

race throughout their lives, noting how we bring more tools to each interaction as we advance in our understanding and embodiment of these dynamics. Building on this work, we sought to look at how two different aspects of identity, one privileged and one oppressed, influence how white women show up in the world.

Our model looks at white women's assumptions, attitudes, and resulting behaviors on a continuum from hegemony to liberation. (If, like us, you have a hard time remembering how to say the word *hegemony*, think of pronouncing it like "Hegemony Cricket" from Disney's Pinocchio.) Hegemony is defined as the dominance of one group or ideology over another. We use this word to indicate the many ways whiteness and patriarchy dictate the dominant, often invisible, rules and codes of power in the United States. In other words, the model documents a progression from full, unquestioning, active participation in a racist, patriarchal capitalist culture to an integrated, socially just way of being.

Throughout the book, we will explore how surviving sexism and benefiting from white privilege results in patterns of behavior common to white women. Some of the characteristics and even full stages we've identified may also show up in white men, in Men and Women of Color, and in gender-nonconforming individuals of all races. We are not saying the examples and stories are exclusive to white women, only that they are patterns most commonly found in white women.

Certainly, patriarchy and white privilege have influenced all of us. Identity development and response pattern models exist for People of Color as well. For example, in her book, *Culture and Power in the Classroom*, Antonia Darder introduces a bicultural developmental framework for People of Color where she describes behavior patterns of *Cultural Alienation, Cultural Separatism, Cultural Dualism, and Cultural Negotiation.*[1] These illustrate how a Person of Color might engage with dominant culture at any given time. Darder's model helps explain how the strategy of divide and conquer results in colorism and internalized oppression where People of Color may harm one another or themselves to get ahead in racist systems. Like with white women, these patterns of engaging don't fit every individual, but they can be helpful to better understand behaviors. It is important to keep in mind that most of the stories shared in this book happen in relationships, where two or more people are interacting with one another and may be understanding the world in very different ways, lending to the complexity of trying to untangle systems of oppression.

Being the buffer between white men and People of Color means most of the beliefs and behaviors we highlight in our identity development model involve having someone else dictate what we should do while holding an inherent sense of superiority over those we are telling what to do. As we develop more consciousness of our sexism and white privilege, the way we maneuver with individuals and within systems changes. Understanding this hierarchical position is key to understanding the indicators of each stage in the model.

The different phases or stages (we use this terminology interchangeably throughout the book) consist of patterns in beliefs and behaviors that illustrate a particular world view and skill set or toolkit. Listed below the name of each of the phases in the diagram is the way white women understand the relationship between racism and sexism at that point in their development. For example, in Immersion, our internalized sense of racial superiority is willful and unquestioned. White women in this stage may actively support racist and sexist laws and demonstrate assumptions about the inherent inferiority of women and People of Color. This overarching way of understanding the world then dictates how we think about issues of race and gender and leads to the patterns we've identified as characteristic of that phase. There are white women who will have many, but not all, of the characteristics identified in a particular stage. When taken together, these indicators signify a particular understanding and way of being in the world.

Conversations in workshops and focus groups and with Colleagues of Color helped us further flesh out the indicators of each stage while confirming our belief in six unique stages. We recognize this as a work in progress and continue to critically examine additions and modifications.

Although white women may see ourselves reflected in many of the phases, we predominantly access the tools of only one most of the time. (And we like to think we're more advanced than we actually are, #winning!) For example, a white woman may have moments of behaviors indicating Balance, where she genuinely connects with another white woman in their struggle for justice, but most of the time she lives in the stage we call Projection and sees other white women as barriers to progress.

In her Human Development course at Pacific Oaks College, Dr. Leticia Nieto also used the metaphor of Russian nesting dolls to describe developmental phases in a way that applies to this model. All white women start with the smallest skill set and least self-awareness, the tiny doll in the center. We don't realize there are larger dolls, i.e., there are optional ways of understanding and responding to sexism and racism. Even as we access other phases on the continuum, growing a larger understanding, this smallest doll is still within us. At any moment, we may revert to this earliest and least expansive way of thinking and/or acting.

We've seen this recently with the number of white women who formed learning pods for their children in response to COVID–19-related school closures. Although we may truly value equal opportunities for all children, when it comes to our babies missing out, we're far less concerned about racial justice.

Overlapping Characteristics

Each phase of development is made up of several characteristics, or behaviors. Some of the characteristics, such as stereotyping, may appear in multiple stages in different ways. The overarching behavior can look the same from the outside, even as the internal motivation changes. For (a real) example, a white woman in Immersion may buy a bandana with images of Native Americans in headdresses and teepees because she likes the design and colors, with no consciousness of the stereotypes. In Defense, she believes wearing this bandana signals her closeness with Indigenous Peoples and distance from her colonizer ancestry and wears it proudly. In Projection, she "ironically" takes pictures of the bandana in a variety of locations, using humor to signify her understanding of how racist the bandana is and how not racist she is. In all three stages, she is unintentionally perpetuating stereotypes in different ways. The impact of white women's behaviors is often the same, as this example illustrates, regardless of our intention or stage of identity development. Even when we're ironically racist in this example, it still serves to bolster our own sense of goodness at the expense of Indigenous Peoples.

It is also not uncommon to move between stages, sometimes within a matter of moments. When we think of the phases as a set of toolboxes as described by Nieto, we can better understand how someone with the ability to use skills in the phase we call Defense might still react with tools more typical of Immersion. When under stress or feeling challenged, particularly when we are challenged around the sense of control we feel entitled to (i.e., our privilege), we may quickly move back and respond less skillfully from an earlier stage of development. As we progress into the stages of Balance and Integration, this happens less often, primarily because we welcome challenges and don't perceive them as an affront to our identity or morality.

For example, if a white woman is in the phase we refer to as Capitulation and someone points out that she got her job through networks having to do with institutional privilege, she may respond with, "You don't know me or my story. I'm a good, hardworking person." Although the person was talking about systems, she responded from a place of individualism, seeing their comment as a personal attack.

When in Balance, she may respond to the same comment with, "Yes, that's a good point. It really bothers me how unfair white privilege is and I'm trying to recognize it more often in my life so I can increase equity in job opportunities for all people. Let's talk more about this." Instead of seeing the comment as a personal affront, she welcomes the conversation that will allow her to be a better ally for justice by working in partnership against white supremacy. Therefore, she is less likely to feel any threat and more likely to use the large toolkit that Nieto references available to her in the Balance stage.

The Progression: Sexism Before White Privilege

All of our lives, the authors have known we are girls, ladies, chicks, gals, women, and this meant we would be seen as less than boys, guys, dudes, men. We've heard the word *woman* itself used as a derogatory term (toward people of all genders). Like most cisgender white women, we were well aware of our gender long before race. Because of this, we developed tools to navigate patriarchy, from pushing back against gender stereotypes to laughing along with sexist jokes. Daily, we use a combination of strategies we've learned and internalized so deeply that often we're unaware of the link between our behaviors and sexism.

Although we are well aware of race when it comes to seeing

People of Color as different, it isn't until later in life, if at all, that white women become aware of our whiteness. The authors grew up in white communities. Tilman lived surrounded by wealth and whiteness in a conservative Washington, DC, suburb. James Loewen identified her hometown as one of the first sundown suburbs in the United States, a place that was an "organized jurisdiction that for decades kept African Americans or other groups from living in it and was thus 'all white.'"[2] People of Color who worked in town, such as the African American woman who raised Tilman, had to be out by sundown if they did not live with their employers. Ilsa lived cocooned by whiteness in a liberal commune in northern Michigan. Although everyone there would say they abhorred racism, we "just happened" to all be white.

We often hear white people say, "I grew up in a white community, so of course I wasn't aware of race." This suggests how normalized whiteness is; so much so that we can be completely surrounded by it and completely oblivious to it. Many white people give up our names, language, and cultural practices that would tie us to our unique European ethnicities when we try to assimilate into the dream of white, American culture. We then bemoan the fact that we have "no culture," not recognizing this was the bargain we made in a power-grab few of us will substantially benefit from. Much like the child who wants to be popular in middle school, we try to minimize our differences and, in so doing, lose some of the strength that comes from knowing who we are.

When we are only surrounded by other white people, denying that whiteness exists at all plays into the narrative of meritocracy used to maintain white supremacy. In other words, we believe our communities are segregated due to differences in our efforts, not, for example, due to racist neighborhood covenants and redlining. We can then reap some benefits of white privilege with no culpability for the harm caused to People of Color.

A white man recently told us, "Race doesn't matter. I know race doesn't impact anyone's life, because it is not something I think about and not something my [white] friends and family talk about." Not only are we unaware we are white, when a Person of Color first tries to point this out to us, but we may also deny it and question the reality of racism in their lives. This then becomes a self-reinforcing cycle. We don't bring up race with People of Color, so we don't think they're talking about race with anyone. People of Color don't talk to us about race because when they do, we don't believe them, which is not a conversation many want to have due to the exhaustion and toll this takes on their lives. We can then easily continue to believe our race doesn't matter.

Because of this, the first three stages in the model include increasing awareness of sexism before white privilege. Some white women will come to a conscious understanding of whiteness before we're aware of the way sexism influences our assumptions and interactions. When this is the case, we are more likely to disregard or accept sexist behavior in racial justice movements.

Most white women will spend their entire lives in the first three phases of development. Getting to the fourth stage, what we call Projection, requires a relationship, an event, or a series of events where we can no longer deny the existence of white privilege. We are at an interesting point in history, where the election of the forty-fifth president and the assassination of George Floyd have been this pivotal moment for many white women. Many of us can't help but recognize the upsurge of blatant white supremacy and racist rhetoric and actions from white men with and without political clout, especially when they feel emboldened enough to invade our capital.

Our model is dynamic and works on a continuum, meaning that movement does not necessarily happen in one direction. White women must be intentional to make regular progress toward Balance and Integration. When we have less energy, it is more comfortable to return to the habituated tools of a phase such as Capitulation to handle a particular situation. After all, wielding a hammer is easier than figuring out how to operate a power drill. This doesn't mean we stay in those earlier phases for good, but it does mean we need to make the choice every day to figure out how to start the path forward again.

Feeling Each Phase

Progressing toward liberation involves integrating mind, body, and spirit. (Stay with us anti-hippie reader.) The way we literally move in each phase both informs and reflects how we think and interact. At the end of each chapter, there is a gesture associated with that phase of development. Resmaa Menakem, in his book *My Grandmother's Hands*, points out, "White-body supremacy doesn't live just in our thinking brains. It lives and breathes in our bodies. As a result, we will never outgrow white-body supremacy just through discussion, training, or anything else that is mostly cognitive. Instead, we need to look to the body—and to the embodied experience of trauma."[3] There are many ways to embody the different stages. We developed these particular gestures as emblematic of each phase in the ways we hold internalized sexism and white superiority simultaneously.

In our trainings, we describe each gesture as instructions, an invitation for "trying on" that phase. We ask the whole group to move about the room if they are able, enacting the gesture while in community with others. We encourage white women reading this to also try out each of the gestures. Silently move around if you are able while embodying each phase. Notice what it reminds you of from your own life. Reflect on how your body feels as you take on this gesture—do you feel tense, awkward, relaxed, giggly? After completing this exercise, stop long enough to consider how you felt about yourself and others as you moved in this way.

Strategic Questions

At the end of each chapter, we've included some questions for white women in this phase to explore. The assumption of strategic questions, based on Fran Peavey's work, is that we have the answers within us if we are guided by questions toward discovering these truths.[4] It is a coaching model that might be used personally by readers for your own growth or in trying to support the further development of your friends and colleagues.

Depending on our phase of development, different questions are needed to help coach us to the next stage. For example, in the Capitulation stage, we intentionally don't ask a question about a time when a white woman noticed herself going along with a racist or sexist act because she does not yet have enough awareness to recognize this in herself. However, that same prompt might work well to propel a woman in what we call Defense to deeper reflection. In other words, the questions in each chapter are designed to engage white women who are operating primarily from that particular phase or world view and cannot yet see what the larger nesting doll can see. We hope this encourages further development on the continuum.

Using a Developmental Model

One of the reasons we value a developmental model is it normalizes different actions we've taken that otherwise may generate guilt or shame. It also allows us to see the potential for growth, to envision new ways of being we hadn't previously contemplated.

Many readers may immediately start trying to identify the different stages that white women they know or they themselves are in. We tend to think of ourselves as further along in our identity development and compare ourselves to others, which often creates distance from one another. This model is useful only in as far as it propels us toward greater equity and justice, toward true collaboration, rather than creating labels to compete with one another. On any particular day or in any given moment, the authors can see ourselves in all of these phases. Honestly recognizing our mistakes without judgment and focusing on shifting patterns of learned behavior frees us to do better next time. It gives us hope.

4

Immersion

I'm under water, can't breathe, and don't know it.

*Karen: a racist white woman who uses her privilege
to demand her own way at the expense of others.*

— Wikipedia

IN THE FIRST STAGE, Immersion, white women are unquestioningly sustaining the status quo where white men are at the pinnacle of power and white women, in a subordinate role, support them in maintaining that position. We call this Immersion because white women are fully immersed in the dominant culture, actively denying or unaware of and not concerned about our white privilege or experiences with sexism. We choose to minimize and ignore the harm our beliefs and actions cause People of Color. We may even feel nurtured by this system and downplay the harm this causes us physically, psychologically, or socially. In believing all our power comes from white men, we abdicate any power that might come from within us.

In Immersion, we collude with our oppression, both on a conscious and unconscious level. As is true in any stage of development, our other marginalized identities will influence when and how we attempt to access white male power. For example, Immersion may look different for a poor, queer, white woman who has internalized that she just needs to buckle up and deal with whatever challenges she faces because, after all, life's not fair. A straight, married white woman might assert that the proper role for a woman is to "stand by your man." In response to claims of sexism, she responds by accusing other women of not wanting to work hard, making too much of something, or fighting against the natural order of things. White women in this stage may believe feminists hate men.

Women or girls in this stage may be active white supremacists. Or they could be living in white communities, participating in white social groups, attending historically white colleges, and electing white candidates while having no analysis of racism and unwittingly contributing to actions that maintain white supremacy. In many cases, our oppressive behaviors *are* intentional, but white women rarely admit our intent is racist. Instead, we hide behind a characteristic that is critical to maintaining patriarchy and white supremacy—our mythical innocence. White men use the protection of our innocence to justify violence against People of Color, and white women assert our innocence to avoid culpability for racist actions.

Because things seem to be going well for us and men are supporting our efforts, we may confidently deny the existence of sexism and how it is playing out in our lives. We may assert that other women who point out sexism are too sensitive. In one of our focus groups, Shelly demonstrated what this characteristic could look like when she said,

> I was like a Title 9 kid who got so many benefits in my world day to day, that I do not feel like in my particular life that any doors have ever been closed to me because I'm a woman. I don't even feel like I internalized the messages at the time of growing up that girls aren't good at math. My female friends working away in Los Angeles, they would be telling me of their particular reactions and tales in meetings where men would do things and they were very quick to pick up on it, where that feels like patriarchy. I didn't have the same resonance of those things...I didn't see it as sexist just because a man did it.

She is well aware of stereotypes of women. And she recognizes laws, such as Title 9, that she benefited from as a woman. In other words, she knows sexism is real. At the same time, she implies her friends' perception of sexism is likely an overreaction to men in general.

White women both actively and passively participate in the oppression of People of Color in the phase we call Immersion. We have internalized and justified our view that the needs and comfort of white people, and especially white men, are paramount. This does not mean most of us wake up and plan to deliberately cause harm to People of Color, but it does mean we wake up with a deep, often unconscious, idea that our whiteness equates with superiority. Our internal sense of white superiority and resulting actions can be obvious to those we interact with but are invisible to the white women exhibiting these behaviors. We may believe we have worked harder, are more intelligent, more well-rounded, more virtuous, and more deserving than People of Color. This belief in our inherent "betterness" is one of the factors that can make it so difficult for us to hear feedback about our racist assumptions.

In one focus group, Peggy captured this when she noted that this is the stage many white women will occupy our whole lives.

> First thing in the morning is a sense of being taken care of by a big power structure that I think I can depend on: heat, light, water, companionship, food, a working car. It's assumed almost to the point that it's part of my identity… I wake up racist. Racism is on my hard drive. And unless I do what I think of as installing the alternative software, I will go through the day just as racist as I began it.

In some cases, white women notice we're exhibiting racist behavior and passively don't care because it feels more comfortable to let things go and create an alternate narrative in our minds. Or we actively don't care because we are focused on a specific goal or agenda. In these moments, we are quite skilled at hijacking or redirecting the conversation when accused of racism. Both of us have used strategies such as defensiveness, anger, sarcasm, hate, disingenuousness, and feigned stupidity in these moments.

For example, when parents of one of her students accused Ilsa of a racist action with their child, she said she couldn't talk with them about it because they confronted her over email and that was the wrong approach. When they asked for a phone call, she said they needed to meet in person for this type of serious discussion. When they tried to schedule a meeting in person, she said it was the end of the school year and she did not have time. Ilsa justified her unwillingness to hear their feedback by claiming they gave the feedback in the wrong way, then put up multiple barriers to meeting in the "right way." She told herself, "Besides, how *dare* they?! I'm a good teacher and they have no idea how hard I work. It's time for my summer vacation." End of story.

Given that we live in a sexist society, sometimes women will strategically use behaviors condoned by white men to advance ourselves. For example, a white woman might think or know she has to flirt or soften her voice to move forward in an industry controlled by men as understood in the patriarchal bargain. Although the behavior may look similar, knowingly making the patriarchal bargain is different from the acquiescence of what we're noticing in the Immersion stage.

Normalizing Whiteness

Immersion is characterized by a monocultural and individualistic perspective. In other words, whiteness is the unquestioned norm, not recognized as a shared group identity. People who are monocultural and individualistic have a difficult time seeing they are part of a larger, white culture (having a collective experience of whiteness). Therefore, we are challenged by the idea that our behavior, which we see as uniquely personal, may be connected to our socialization and social locations as white people. White women in Immersion are often offended by the word "white" itself, protesting against being referred to by this classification with a group, rather than just being seen as individuals or Americans. The more oppression we experience daily because of our religion, age, class, etc., in addition to our gender, the harder it may be to see any privileges we get from whiteness.

In contrast, Melissa V. Harris-Perry writes how Black people can't help but recognize their group racialization because they have been targeted as a collective, not individuals. "American racial terror was predicated on precisely this unwillingness to distinguish among Black people. Terrorism targets its victims not for their actions but for their identity. African Americans developed a keen sense of how individual behavior was linked to collective susceptibility."[1] Their very survival depends on understanding whiteness.

This difference in experience and worldview leads to social divisions and furthers racial segregation. Ilsa noted,

> While my best friend in junior high was Black, we never discussed race. And even as we obsessed over boys, my friend never dated anyone. I assumed we had the same experience in school, were given equal opportunity by teachers and classmates. Racism existed in the south or the inner city, not in the suburbs, especially since my friend came from a wealthy family.

While Ilsa wasn't noticing race, her friend was undoubtedly aware of the social cost of Blackness in the predominantly white suburbs, from standards of attractiveness and acceptability, to access to gifted classes. White women's denial of the reality of our racialized experience is one of the challenges to interracial relationships in the Immersion phase. We do not believe People of Color who share their experiences with racism, because we assume everyone has the same reality, a white reality, regardless of race.

Therefore, if People of Color are being mistreated, white women in the Immersion phase usually assume it is because of something they have brought on themselves. If a Person of Color calls out racism, we may react by asking, "Why is everything *always* about race?" or accuse them of "playing the race card" to try to get out of personal responsibility. Reacting to videos showing police targeting Black people, we may respond with, "Why didn't she just do what he asked? Why did he run away if he was innocent? I would have…." We don't recognize that the assumption of our innocence means we experience a different reality with law enforcement.

This individualistic way of thinking is taught to us through the bootstrap myth of meritocracy. Work hard and get ahead. In liberal circles it is reinforced through magical thinking: You manifest or make your reality.

White women have historically been and are currently regarded as the "norm" or ideal of what it means to be a woman. This impacts Women of Color in a multitude of ways. Skin bleaching cream is a billion-dollar international business. Not infrequently, Women of Color are rendered invisible in discussions of gender pay equity, where the "average" pay of women doesn't reflect the disparities along racial lines. This is also true for violence against women. For example, Indigenous women in the US are more than twice as likely to experience violence than any other demographic group, and the homicide rate of Indigenous women in Canada was six times as high compared to other women.[2] Yet the data regarding violence against women are rarely disaggregated to tell the truth about our different realities. White women in the Immersion stage are oblivious to the ways their identity and worldview are centered in defining what it means to be a woman. At the same time, Women of Color are often portrayed as hypersexual and deserving of violence, the diametric opposite of the stereotype of white innocence.

Gender Role Limitations

Because of the norming of whiteness, most white women will be aware of their gender much earlier than their race. We learn socially constructed, sanctioned gender roles from a young age that are designed to augment the power of white patriarchy. Ilsa's definition of woman/girl was always in reaction to what it meant to be a man/boy.

> When I was young, I refused to wear pink because it was a "girl" color, and I didn't want to be seen as "girly." I knew

the confines of that gender role. Alternatively, I was told (and felt) I looked beautiful when, as a seven-year-old, I wore a full-length purple velvet renaissance-era dress to the movies. To this day I catch myself complimenting women more on their appearance when they're wearing a skirt or dress versus pants.

Like many girls growing up in the 1960s and 1970s, Tilman and Ilsa were unaware of genders beyond the false boy/girl binary, so never questioned the idea that their identity and gender expression would fall into one or the other category.

Ilana teased out the tendency to conflate sexual orientation and gender identity: "I often feel like LGB (lesbian, gay, bisexual) is one sort of set and then genderism and sexism are inextricably linked. Because even though I am cisgender and experience gender privilege, there are still gender expectations in the world, in a gender binary policing world, that I have to conform to in order to be accepted. In order to be respected. In order to be everything right? So, my gender is being policed."

Terrie shared a story of the cost of gender policing when she faked an injury just to be able to wear pants at a time when girls were expected to wear skirts or dresses.

I went to school in pants two days in a row and I said, 'I have to wear pants today because I injured my legs and I have to keep them warm.' I remembered limping; it was all fake. And then the next day it was gym, and it was like, 'Oh fuck.' It's gym and I can't participate in gym. I have to lie here with my leg up and everybody's having fun. And that's Immersion. It's like having to choose between one kind of behavior and another, one kind of dress and another, one kind of consequence and another. The consequence of getting in trouble or being the troublemaker.

Because we access our privilege by not breaking rules and not being seen as troublemakers, white women like Terrie try to find ways to appear to go along, even when we'd rather not. In this stage, internalized sexism shows up in the choice between two consequences.

We may buy into heteronormative roles of white women and girls, i.e., the dainty little lady who would never wear pants to school and whose greatest aspiration is to marry a rich man. As Peggy said, "I knew I wanted to get married and of course I would find Mr. Right and then he would take care of me for the rest of my life. So, Mr. Right in a position to take care of me for the rest of my life had to have money." Which also means he's white and looks a lot like Prince Charming.

Or we may distance ourselves from other women, trying to not be seen as stereotypically female. Instead of critiquing the system of sexism, we internalize sexism and critique other women.

Mallory spoke about this.

> I didn't feel comfortable with male and female roles growing up and rebelled against my femaleness because I didn't know there was another way to be female. And so, I was always dressing in the wrong clothes and dirty and playing with bugs and spiders and worms and digging. So, any woman who tried to attach herself to me was messing with my thing, right. It was messing with my reputation and sullying it. I'm going to be seen as other girls are seen, as silly and brainless and not brave and not adventurous. [I made] attempts to isolate myself from lesser beings and try to identify with the guys.

These examples also speak to how whiteness is connected to gender expectations of girls and women. Sojourner Truth famously pointed out in her speech "Ain't I a Woman?" how men trying to keep women from working, protecting their virtue, and seeing them as dainty had never been her norm. Black women had always done back-breaking labor.

> That man over there say.
> A woman needs to be helped into carriages
> And lifted over ditches

And to have the best place everywhere.
Nobody ever helped me into carriages
Or over mud puddles
Or gives me a best place…
Ain't I a woman?[3]

What gets named as "traditional" gender roles are roles of white women. Tilman grew up in a community with these expectations.

> I was born into an upper-class family in the late 1950s, and white women's traditional gender roles were the norm for the white women I was surrounded by. I went to school, dance classes, cultural and social events to learn just enough (but not too much) to be an asset to a future husband. A main point of my education was to position me to be a viable spouse for a powerful white man and, ultimately, to do his bidding, as necessary. I was raised to understand that my thoughts, needs, and values are secondary to the needs of the men in my sphere.

Another assumption in this stage is that women are to serve men in whatever capacity needed, no matter how smart the women are, and especially if we are smarter. The "payoff" is that the white women are given economic and social security and, most importantly, proximity to power if we play our part in the game.

The Carrot and the Stick

White women stay in Immersion because of both the rewards of privilege we receive for going along with patriarchy and white supremacy and the threat of exclusion and losing access to privilege if we do not. This can lead many of us to suppress the fullness of who we are for fear of punishment. This is particularly true when we have a marginalized identity we can keep hidden to some degree. For example, Ilsa let her peers believe she was straight through high school and even convinced herself of this false narrative at times. This protected her from social exclusion and the threat of violent homophobia.

Institutions and individuals give carrots to white women for staying immersed in their internalized white superiority, sexism, and heteronormativity or traditional gender roles in male/female relationships. The reward may be in the form of a perceived sense of safety. Johanna reflected on her childhood:

> I remembered that I was happy with traditional roles with regard to here's what the man does and here's what the woman does. That worked for me. It was comfortable. It made me happy. I think it felt like safety... And I remember throughout my childhood that if my mom and dad were in an argument I would think, "She should quit pushing him." If only she would be quiet because he was the man of the house. I grew up with him sitting at the kitchen table in his chair while I got him his iced tea, and Momma's making his dinner, and he was the decision maker, and it was all that traditional gender role stuff. I wished she would just shut up because he was upset, and she was going to further upset him.

White women in the phase of Immersion will often respond by shaming other white women when they see them pushing "too hard" on the white men in their lives. It is much simpler to go along.

Mallory shared a pattern in her childhood that would appear each time her father lost a job. Instead of coming home with the bad news and figuring out the next steps together, her father would bring home a steak. That would be the signal that they'd have dinner and bring out the moving boxes. No one questioned this behavior or considered renegotiating it. Mallory's mom knew what was expected and acted in accordance.

The desire to fit in and not make waves is a part of the conditioning of sexism for white women; be nice especially to white men and keep their egos intact. Support your man even when it is not in your best interest. The imparting of these values happens from a young age, as we watch our mothers, sisters, and other female role models teach us the man's sense that he is okay and in control is more important than family economic realities, quality of life, and/or a woman's well-being. Cornell philosophy professor Kate Mann coined the term *himpathy* as "the inappropriate and disproportionate sympathy powerful men often enjoy in cases of sexual assault, intimate partner violence, homicide and other misogynistic behavior."[4] This perfectly names the worldview of white women in the phase of Immersion.

We also learn to not be too nice to People of Color for fear of people getting the wrong idea about us caring about them. Recognizing the threat of association, white women may distance ourselves from People of Color when it appears to others as if we are too closely related or chummy. Mallory shared a story of how she was taught to internalize this as a young girl under the threat of social isolation or violence from her peers:

> There's a defining experience when an African American woman came to work at my elementary school and most of the kids in the school had never seen an African American before. Her last name was Clark, the same as mine. And it was an incident where I became the focus of a lot of nasty…I just remember being backed up against a portable with people screaming at me. This ring of faces all contorted. Yelling about how I was related to her because we had the same last name. And I kept saying I have an "e" at the end of my name, and she doesn't, we're not related!

Without realizing why, Mallory was intimidated into defending against any kind of relationship with her African American teacher.

When we do not comply with the rules of the dominant society, whether intentionally or by happenstance, we are sanctioned. White women from wealthy families, such as Tilman's, face the "stick" of disinheritance. We would have to give up generations of wealth collected on the backs of People of Color and Indigenous land and labor, should we decide not to collude with sexism and racism in our families.

Mallory reflects on how white power was enforced in her childhood and the consequences of not complying.

[W]e moved to New Orleans and it was 1964. One of the images is of me standing in front of my church where these windows just went forever. It's really beautiful, but there's bullet holes in them. And there's a policeman there and we have to go to church under armed guard for about three-quarters of a year. This changed my perspective on what my country was. And who I was.

The reason we were attacked was we were an integrated congregation and many of the people in the church were helping to walk a young girl from her house to the elementary school near her house, which was an all-white elementary school, and she was integrating that school. She needed protection and the adults in my church did that, along with a lot of other things. People shot in the back window of the minister's car and firebombed his house. I was twelve or thirteen when all of that started. It had a huge impact on me.

Although Mallory's response to this was to embrace a lifetime of activism, many white women who face direct or indirect threats will internalize fear and subordination. We learn that the cost of standing up against racism and sexism is too high. And we may get the rewards of wealth, friendships, and the perception of safety when we go along with white male superiority. Understanding this, we can see why white women may abdicate their own agency, both consciously and unconsciously.

Advancing White Male Agendas

White supremacy and patriarchy dictate that our self-worth comes from our objective value to white men. In the Immersion stage, we believe this to be true. Peggy described a skit she wrote illustrating behaviors and school curricula in a similar phase:

Phase one is the all-white, womanless curriculum [in school]...Women are invisible. [For the skit] I am introduced as Mrs. Kenneth McIntosh...and I'm dressed all up as the little lady under the protection of my husband. And the introduction is all about my father's achievements and my husband's achievements, and then I come in as Mrs. Kenneth McIntosh.

The white woman in this phase willingly makes her needs invisible and derives her identity from her husband.

White men often use white women in the phase we call Immersion to promote and prop up their political and economic agendas by having them message and perpetuate stereotypes of People of Color and other white women. The buffer zone provides a great lever. White women justify the "need" for white male supremacy to make important decisions on behalf of the nation.

Sarah Palin deliberately played this role for the Republican Party and John McCain in 2012 and more recently for Donald Trump. She asked during a rally endorsing Trump on January 19th, 2016,

> Are you ready to make America great again? We all have a part in this. We all have a responsibility. Looking around at all of you, you hard-working Iowa families. You farm families, and teachers, and teamsters, and cops, and cooks. You rocking rollers. And holy rollers! All of you who work so hard. You full-time moms. You with the hands that rock the cradle... Are you ready for a commander-in-chief who will let our warriors do their job and go kick ISIS' ass?[5]

Her assertion that somehow these hardworking people will benefit from their sons going to war served as a dog whistle to white people everywhere to perpetuate the reality of United States imperialism and white supremacy.

The unique intersection of internalized sexism (doing a white man's bidding willingly) and internalized white supremacy (believing we need to be in charge) are used to keep white men paramount at the expense of everyone else. Phyllis Schlafly demonstrated this in the 1970s when she used her time and intellect to organize against the Equal Rights Amendment. Male politicians who disregarded her political activism in other arenas welcomed her work against women's rights.

White men have no intention of sharing power with these women, and as soon as they have served their purpose, the women quickly disappear. These may be smart, competent women, but their primary role is to lure supporters to their cause using a combination of sharp language, sexiness, and/or fierceness. The way they dress, wear their hair, and defer when necessary are all components of the phase we call Immersion, and are carefully crafted to solicit support for powerful white male agendas.

Trump has used this strategy well in his campaign and presidency. Hope Hicks, Kelly Anne Conway, Kristjen Neilsen, Nikki Halley, and Betsy DeVoss have all been mouthpieces for Trump, almost always making policy that clearly benefits white male corporations over American citizens. A clear example of this dynamic is illustrated by his former press secretary Sarah Huckabee Sanders. Sanders came to Trump's election campaign when Trump asked her father, Mike Huckabee, for an endorsement. Huckabee suggested that Trump enlist his daughter since he needed a stronger link to evangelicals and women. Sanders was happy to provide that link. She, along with the two press secretaries who followed her, faithfully stood at her podium representing the president no matter how egregious his words or actions. As an article in *The New Yorker* observed,

> Watching Sanders at the podium, it is difficult to discern her personal feelings about the most inflammatory aspects of Trump's agenda—she likes to say that it is her job to "state policy, not make policy." She has never betrayed disappointment in the President's personal behavior or offensive remarks. After the white-supremacist violence in Charlottesville, Virginia, Trump was broadly condemned for insisting that there had been 'blame' on all sides. When Sanders addressed those remarks, she echoed his equivocation: "The President's been very outspoken in his condemnation of racism and bigotry and hate of all forms."[6]

Sanders' job was to deflect for her boss and to attract white female and evangelical supporters and voters for him. While she claimed that reporters have been personally tough on her, *The New Yorker* continues, "Sanders might not actually be hoping for more decorousness from the press corps. The campaign strategist in her surely realizes that heated exchanges generally work to Trump's advantage. The more aggressive the press's questions, the more loudly the president cries 'fake news,' and the more tenaciously his base supports him. It's also been good for Sanders's job security: the more ferociously she responds to the media in public, the more Trump admires her."

Huckabee Sanders got her power first from her governor father and then from the United States president. She placed herself with powerful white men and ran their agendas for them in order to fulfill her own conservative agenda.

Competing for Male Attention

In this stage, white women may compete with other women for the attention of men. Even though some white women are not interested in male sexual attention, they may still compete for accolades and access to power via white men. As Johanna illustrated, "In particular I wanted the attention of older white men, like my male teachers." We believe our value derives from how white men see and treat us.

Dena spoke about the importance of her relationships with white men:

> I look back at when I was a kid and being a lesbian was so bad and so wrong that I never even got to explore the possibility that I could be a lesbian. And I am, by the way. But I really see it as this sort of dominant, hegemonic, oppressive whiteness that has gotten us into this trouble that we're in. And so literally who I was attracted to, it not only had to be male but a white male. It wasn't an option. Nothing else was an option.

White women also may exercise internalized superiority to one-up Women of Color in our competition to get this attention and the rewards it brings. Women of Color are generally excluded from the competition for white men from the start—rendered undesirable or invisible compared to the white beauty norms. This was true for Ilsa's friend who never dated in junior high. Our competition with Women of Color is like swimming laps and deciding we're racing the person in the next lane over. Although that person never knew they were in a race, we wear ourselves out trying to pass them and "win."

As a Black woman recently told us, "I'm doing me. You do you." In just trying to get by, she didn't have the time or energy for white women's perceived competition. Johanna noted this in her experience in high school, "There was just no need to compete with [Women of Color] and I realize that today. That will make me get upset because that's just so dehumanizing. But…they just weren't a part of that equation because of the racism that was part of my community."

Katy had a different experience going to a high school that was less than fifty percent white. As she pointed out, the commodifying of Men of Color and the view of scarce resources, i.e., good men, fed the competition between women. She came face to face with anger from Black women directed at white women for stealing all of the good men.

> The anger came back at us, white women, if we were dating a Man of Color. We were obviously kind of sneaking like the weasel in the henhouse concept. Like we're doing some magic. But the racism piece is, I [as a white woman] can look down on you and your choices. Your fashion choices, your language choices, your hair and go, 'Well no wonder…If Black women don't want to lose their men then don't be such a bitch.' So that was my way of protecting myself from the anger, by blaming back because I felt defensive. I mean I wasn't even dating Men of Color, but it

was just in the water. It wasn't like there was an interaction of it coming straight at me but just this concept of, "Mine. Property. Stay away." And I blamed back because I didn't understand.

In Immersion, we don't see institutional racism, so we often blame the victims. Katy's internalized superiority told her she was better than the Black women in her school. This worldview of individualizing and objectifying, without recognizing oppressive systems, keeps women and girls competing with one another and ultimately upholds patriarchy and white supremacy.

In her essay, *Poetry is not a Luxury*, Audre Lorde provides a helpful analysis of this dynamic.

> War, imprisonment, and "the street" have decimated the ranks of black males of marriageable age. The fury of many black heterosexual women against white women who date black men is rooted in this unequal sexual equation within the black community, since whatever threatens to widen that equation is deeply articulated and resented. But this is essentially unconstructive resentment because it extends sideways only. It can never result in true progress on the issue because it does not question the vertical lines of power or authority, nor the sexist assumptions which dictate the terms of that competition...Black women are programmed to define ourselves within this male attention and to compete with each other for it rather than to recognize and move upon our common interests.[7]

In order to more fully understand this anger, there are many vertical lines of power and authority that white women must learn. For example, we would need to be aware of racist beauty standards that rank us the prettiest and most desirable, and if not, certainly the most socially and symbolically valuable. We would have to understand the stereotypes Black women face of being overly sexual, the Jezebel myth as Melissa Harris-Perry names this, and, therefore, not suitable for long-term relationships.[8] In Immersion, there is no systemic analysis, so white women lash out or blame back, as in Katy's case.

The Ideal Object

Whiteness is one of the standards of beauty and acceptability; of what it means to be an "ideal woman." As such, white women can fit traditional sexist stereotypes. Laura talked about having to prove her intelligence when people found out she was a stay-at-home mom. While she would get the almost sympathetic message, "Oh your blonde hair, blue eyes and you don't work, you must not have any education," she knew this was in stark contrast to Black women who are stereotyped as "welfare queens" who are milking the system if they stay home to care for their children.

As white women in Immersion strive for this ideal, Chris points out how problematic it is:

> You know what this gets you when you fit the ideal woman? It gets you raped. You are the ideal possession…You are not a person. And when I look sexy like that, people are not interested in me because I'm smart. They're not interested in anything I have to say…But I don't feel like there's a lot of talk about what happens when you're the ideal object. And what you have to give up and what you lose when you are the ideal object. Yes, you gain power. It's a certain kind of power and it comes at a cost.

Out of positioning white women as the ideal possession, white men could justify the rape of white women. It was also codified by law and social norms that raping Black and Indigenous women was not possible. Rape in marriage was legal in every US state until the 1970s. It wasn't until 1993 (the year Ilsa graduated from high school!) that all states had withdrawn the legal exemption of marital rape.

This also set the stage for the myth of the Black rapist. Lisa Lindquist-Dorr, associate professor at the University of Alabama, explained this myth that dominated white, Southern culture, saying, "Sexual access to women is a trophy of power, white women embodied virtue and morality, they signified whiteness and white superiority, so sexual access to white women was possessing the ultimate privilege that white men held. It makes women trophies to be traded among men."

The stereotype of the pure, virginal white woman who is coveted by all men juxtaposed next to the stereotype of the untamed, untrustworthy Black man, played a huge part in setting up the rationale for lynching and murdering African American men. As Linquist Dorr asserts,

> After Reconstruction, whites conflated Black men's desires for white women with their desire for political rights as men, thus creating the rape myth. By the twentieth century, the rape myth was at its height, and it structured most white southerners' beliefs about the consequences of allowing interaction between White women and Black men. The rhetoric about Black men's propensity to rape and the corresponding need for white men to protect white women flourished both in debates about Black men's civil and political rights and in discussions about new freedoms and opportunities for White women. The rape myth thus enforced white women's subordination to white men and the social, economic, and political power of whites over Blacks.[9]

Ida B. Wells-Barnett put her own life at great risk to fight lynching laws. In her book, *Southern Horrors: Lynch Law in All Its Phases*, she described a case where a white woman accused a Black man of rape after consensual sex, in order to preserve her reputation.

> The *Cleveland Gazette* of January 16, 1892, publishes a case in point. Mrs. J. S. Underwood, the wife of a minister of Elyria, Ohio, accused an Afro-American of rape. She told her husband that during his absence in 1888, stumping the State for the Prohibition Party, the man came to the kitchen door, forced his way in the house and insulted her. She tried to drive him out with a heavy poker, but he

overpowered and chloroformed her, and when she revived her clothing was torn and she was in a horrible condition. She did not know the man but could identify him. She pointed out William Offett, a married man, who was arrested and, being in Ohio, was granted a trial.

The prisoner vehemently denied the charge of rape, but confessed he went to Mrs. Underwood's residence at her invitation and was criminally intimate with her at her request. This availed him nothing against the sworn testimony of a minister's wife, a lady of the highest respectability. He was found guilty, and entered the penitentiary, December 14, 1888, for fifteen years. Sometime afterwards the woman's remorse led her to confess to her husband that the man was innocent.[10]

These are her words:

I met Offett at the Post Office. It was raining. He was polite to me, and as I had several bundles in my arms, he offered to carry them home for me, which he did. He had a strange fascination for me, and I invited him to call on me. He called, bringing chestnuts and candy for the children. By this means we got them to leave us alone in the room. Then I sat on his lap. He made a proposal to me and I readily consented. Why I did so, I do not know, but that I did is true. He visited me several times after that and each time I was indiscreet. I did not care after the first time. In fact, I could not have resisted, and had no desire to resist.

When asked by her husband why she told him she had been outraged, she said: "I had several reasons for telling you. One was the neighbors saw the fellows here, another was, I was afraid I had contracted a loathsome disease, and still another was that I feared I might give birth to a Negro baby. I hoped to save my reputation by telling you a deliberate lie."

To this day, white men continue to use white women's safety to justify the murder of People of Color. When Dylann Roof killed nine Black people at the Emmanuel AME church in South Carolina, according to an eye witness he stated, "You rape our women and you're taking over our country."[11] Situating white women as the ideal object needing protection is another example of the buffer zone in maintaining white male power.

Nice White Ladies Hurting People of Color

It is relatively easy to point out white women in the stage of Immersion who have demonstrated white supremacy in obvious ways. However, these are not the only women who do day-to-day harm to People of Color.

White women may go into helping professions with the desire to provide services for People of Color. In Immersion, we frequently hold paternalistic beliefs that Families of Color could not survive, much less thrive, without our support and interventions on their behalf.

Well-meaning white women often make decisions and judgments that ultimately have racist consequences. Being "good people" doesn't preclude us from this reality. Tilman shared this experience to illustrate her collusion with sexism and white privilege.

When my first baby was just two months old, I was asked to bring him across the country to attend my parents' forty-fifth wedding anniversary party. I did this with trepidation because I had purposely moved far away from my family to distance myself from what I had experienced to be an abusive environment. But my love for my father, combined with my internalized sense of what it meant to be a good daughter by not upsetting our traditional family values won over, and I agreed to go.

The evening of the celebration brought specific challenges for me because I was told I wasn't allowed to bring my baby to the party, which countered my values and intuition as a mother. I was breast-feeding him exclusively at the time, and he wasn't experienced with bottles, so I was especially nervous about leaving him behind. I tried to find an old friend whom I could trust to watch him for me but was unsuccessful. I was coached and cajoled into agreeing to have a professional babysitting service send someone over to watch him during the evening. I felt anxious, guilty, and angry that I was in this situation. The only solace I had was to imagine what kind of wonderful woman would arrive at my door to alleviate all of my anxieties. She was white. She was matronly. She was resolutely middle class.

At the appointed time, the doorbell rang, and I looked out the window to catch a glimpse of the babysitter. I am not sure what my physical response was, but my brain went into hyper mode. The woman I saw was African American, young, thin, dressed in what I considered to be a slinky dress with high platform shoes, and a big afro. Without knowing one thing about this woman, before I even opened the door, I was deeply in Immersion, and no part of me thought she would be appropriate or competent to take care of my precious baby.

My immediate response to this woman was to resent the agency for sending her to *this house*, in *this particular neighborhood*. I felt let down by the agency for not "knowing better." This neighborhood dictated specific kinds of babysitters, meaning white.

But I had been directed that I needed to be at this party and that my baby could not come, so I very tentatively left them together; leaving many directives, asking invasive questions, making many passive-aggressive comments. I spent the party worried and resentful, and called the sitter regularly. After so many calls, she finally told me that my son wouldn't stop crying and I needed to come home. Even though I was relieved to be able to leave the party, I also felt (wrongly) vindicated in that she wasn't able to perform to my expectations. This confirmed in my mind that I was not stereotyping her, she really was the problem, allowing me to maintain my steadfast self-image as not racist.

Part of me knew that I was being racist, and I didn't want to admit it, so I cloaked my racism in "niceness" with this woman. I insincerely blamed myself for being a new mother and "overprotective" when I was really just worried about leaving my child with her. The tiny part of me that I allowed to see this was a hostile situation for her from the beginning, and that I was lacking empathy for her reality, was buried in my racism. My internalized sexism propelled me to go to the party, and my internalized white superiority propelled me to treat her in racist ways and then try to fake that I was being kind. We both knew I was lying, but it was never said out loud.

I felt caught between meeting the needs of my family and meeting the needs of myself and my son; I should have just said no to my family, but I didn't. Instead, I felt resentful about my situation, and someone was going to pay. So, I took this out on someone else who had less power than I.

Tilman's story indicates the lack of agency white women may assert in Immersion. We passively go along with the white male agenda and then take out our frustrations on People of Color with less power. We might posit we had no choice or simply use passive language to describe our collusion, absolving us of responsibility, but this very intentional "unintentional" version of racism and sexism is no less harmful to People of Color and women.

Final Thoughts

The legacy of white women actively engaging in racist rhetoric and actions for white men, or hiding behind racist assumptions to protect ourselves, is a key component of our internalized sexism and white superiority. Many white women don't want to move out of this stage. A characteristic of Immersion is to deny that any other way of being is desirable. We're perfectly happy, we tell ourselves and anyone who cares to listen.

The pain of having to accept the reality of sexism from (white) men and the regular practice of dehumanizing People of Color both cut us deeply and can affect our physical, emotional, and spiritual well-being. Many white women in Immersion will put up walls and create alternative narratives to protect ourselves from our woundedness and maintain our sense of control, coming across as cold and callous. This is the time when we need the most support and critical feedback from other white women to help us navigate through our racist and sexist assumptions. Recognizing we are immersed and moving forward takes humility and honesty.

Feeling Immersion

As referenced in the introduction, each stage includes a gesture to help readers embody this way of being.

Sit up, or if you can, stand tall. Pull your shoulders back. Lift your chin and imagine you are looking down your nose at other people. Take quick, shallow breaths, never fully inhaling or exhaling. As you move around, you might give a knowing wink, particularly to a man. Never look a white man directly in the eye unless trying to seduce him. Envision looking other women, trans or nonbinary people, and Men of Color up and down. Maintain a physical distance of at least three feet from any other person.

- As you held this gesture, what felt natural to you? What felt unnatural?
- What feelings came up for you? Where did these feelings land in your body?
- If you were with other women when you tried this gesture, how did their bodies feel and look to you? How did you feel toward them?

Strategic Questions for Immersion

The skill set for engaging in conversations about racism is so limited in this stage that it can be difficult to even bring up race or gender without getting a defensive response. It is important to be strategic in coaching someone in this stage to help them gain a new understanding.

When thinking of any of the stories above, consider these questions:

- Have you ever gone along with something a white man asked you to do, even when you didn't want to? Why?
- How were gender roles defined in your family? Did this ever feel unfair to you? When and how?
- What were the narratives and experiences about race you learned and heard growing up? What were your reactions?
- How do you feel when you hear a story about white women doing racist things?
- How might you support any of the women in the stories above?
- What do you wish the white women in these situations might have done instead?
- Have you ever been in similar situations? What did you do? What do you wish you had done differently?

* my dad
* Daycare @ PDXconference

5

Capitulation

The fear of being alone, or of being unloved,
had caused women of all races to passively accept
sexism and sexist oppression.

— bell hooks

WHITE WOMEN in this stage are aware of, and passively accept, patriarchy and racism. We call it Capitulation because of the willingness to go along to get along with systems of oppression. Capitulation involves abdicating any power or personal agency we might have, then asserting we had no choice.

The main difference between Immersion and Capitulation lies in our awareness of the reality of sexism. In a paper written about Belenky et al.'s *Women's Ways of Knowing*, Pamela Bailey captures the "Subjective Knowledge Phase," one of the four stages of women's development that Belenky and her co-authors conceptualize.

> The woman begins to accept that she has a voice, "an inner source of strength" lying within herself, and an opinion that is due to past experiences. She recognizes that she does not have to agree with the authority but is still cautious about voicing opinions. Truth is experienced within oneself but not acted upon for fear of jeopardizing the associations one has with others at the same level.[1]

While beginning to understand we are harmed by sexism, white women in this stage feel even less agency when it comes to addressing racism. Empathy for People of Color takes a back seat to the immediate sting we often feel from sexism. We generally disregard our own white privilege as a myth. As a result, we often replicate white patriarchal systems in an effort to counter sexism. In so doing, we maintain and perpetuate the degree of privilege we possess.

Although we may notice disadvantages People of Color have, we attribute institutional barriers to individual failures. For example, we might say, "Some families just don't care as much about education." Or, on the liberal side, "Those poor Latinx families are so hard working; they just don't have time to help their children in school." White women in Capitulation won't acknowledge that institutional racism and stereotypes create barriers for People of Color in accessing the educational system or our own unearned advantages as white people that have helped us advance in these same systems. This holds true in all institutions. We support assimilation to the dominant culture's norms and values.

The legacy of institutional racism has made it possible for most white women to grow up in the United States without having many (if any) friendships and social interactions with People of Color. This means most white women in Capitulation do not have personal relationships that might give us any alternate insights on the effects of racism. Instead, we keep our sense of entitlement to privilege and our awareness of sexism we experience at the center of our realities. In other words, I'm the center of my universe.

Putting People of Color at Risk

Because of our lack of attention to racism, it is easy for white women in Capitulation to put People of Color at risk. When lecturing about mass incarceration, Michelle Alexander asks, "How many people in the room have never committed a crime?" From jaywalking, to smoking pot, to shoplifting a pack of gum, most of us have done something illegal at some point. Alexander uses this to illustrate the criminalization of Black and Brown bodies and the assumption of the innocence of white people.

Living a lifetime of being assumed innocent, white women fail to recognize that the danger People of Color face from law enforcement, even when we are with them. Robin shared,

[A Black man and I] were doing training up in a small town…So, we went out to the mall, and we were in Target. And you know in Target they have the area that has the jewelry and watches and things like that? And often there's nobody back there, you know you want to see something but there's nobody back there?

There was this watch I wanted to see in the case, and I was waiting and waiting. I was feeling put out. Come on. I wanted to see that watch and I wanted someone to come over there and serve me. And finally, I just reached down, and my thought was, 'I should not have to reach in here!' I'm righteously reaching in.

And you know where this is going right? The Black guy next to me had a kind of visceral reaction. He was just shaking. Oh my God the contrast between us.

For me, I was feeling self-righteous and for him, it's like something really bad might happen to me right now. And I thought that guy could have been thrown on the ground… And maybe we were already being watched because we were together. I put him at risk without ever thinking about it.

Her sense of entitlement to service, without any regard to the difference in the impact her actions might have on her colleague, illustrates white privilege. Experiences with sexism and classism may have exacerbated her feelings of being put out by having to wait. Although Robin recognized it in the moment, women in Capitulation will minimize or invalidate the experiences of People of Color. We would be more likely to question him with indignation, "Why are you so upset? You didn't reach in the case."

Stuck in the Middle with You

While white men widely hold similar beliefs about the personal or community deficits of People of Color, white women are the majority of the people providing services to those labeled "less fortunate." As we mentioned earlier, intentionally situated as a buffer between white men and People of Color, we are the majority of early childhood professionals, educators, nurses, teachers, and nonprofit workers. It is our role as enforcers of institutional rules in communities we aim to serve that can be particularly problematic for People of Color.

In Capitulation, white women's desire to see ourselves primarily as smart and competent (albeit victims of sexism), and as good people, restrains us from thinking critically about a system that privileges us at the expense of People of Color. Our internalized sexism and desire to achieve with the help of white men can keep us from speaking up for fear of upsetting the patriarchal structure and risking losing some of our privileges as a result.

Tilman's story illustrates an experience of using white norms to provide services to Children of Color.

> One of the first and most concrete experiences happened some thirty years ago when I was a preschool teacher. I thought I was a good teacher—hard working, smart, loving, creative. I deliberately became an early childhood educator in order to introduce the idea of equity and anti-racism to young children. And then one day, one of my student's parents, an African American woman, approached me to ask if she could talk to me. She explained she had been observing me closely and could no longer stay quiet. She described to me how I was disciplining the Students of Color, and especially her daughter, more harshly than the white students in my class.
>
> What a risk this mother took with me. She knew I would be defensive (I was) and dismissive (I was), but she was incredibly patient and gave me huge grace. She didn't do this because she thought I was the benevolent person I thought I was. She did this to protect her child, and probably other children, from my racism.
>
> In this situation, I approached my teaching and my interaction with this mother and child as if everyone reared their children the way I would and the way I was taught— the "normal, developmentally appropriate" way. I assumed I knew better even though I did not have children of my own, and I knew nothing about raising Children of Color

in a racist society. I centered my needs and values to the detriment of her daughter and other Children of Color in my class. My vision of myself as a good and hardworking person prevented me from hearing and believing this mother's critique. It was due to her patience and fortitude with me that I was eventually willing to be curious about what she had told me.

Many educators or white women in other helping professions will never get to the point of believing this critique. In the stage we call Capitulation, we continue to perceive the people giving us feedback as flawed and, therefore, just making excuses for their own poor judgment or lack of parenting skills. We use this narrative to justify making decisions for and holding power over them.

Normalization of the White Woman

As in the stage of Immersion, white women in Capitulation view ourselves as "normal women." Our image gets defined as what it means to be pretty, to be a mother, to be a feminist. We have deeply internalized that the way we do things is the way all people do things (or should do things).

Ilsa shared the following story:

In college, I'd been working in student services with a Black woman. A group of us stopped by her parents' house with her to pick something up. I remember feeling a jarring moment when I looked at all of the pictures on the walls of only Black people. Sure, I knew she was Black, and of course her family's pictures were of their Black relatives. So, what surprised and unsettled me?

I believe this was one of the first times when I had been in a space that didn't center whiteness. Even as our work group was racially diverse, I had still subconsciously categorized her as white. The degree to which my mind assimilated people into white dominant culture became evident in that moment. And my discomfort in a space that didn't cater to me explicitly was palpable.

We may expect our way of life to be central to everyone's experiences and become unsettled when it is not. In Capitulation, we don't recognize this is happening, we simply have a feeling that something's not right and may quickly react in a way that soothes our discomfort. Our internalized white superiority tells us that our way is the right way, even when provided evidence to the contrary.

Peggy offered another example of this, "I was astonished when a Black colleague at University of Denver told me, just in casual conversation, 'I wouldn't want to be white if you paid me a million dollars.' The fact that I was astonished showed that I had really internalized that whites were superior. I had assumed that my life was much better than hers."

In Capitulation, white women are pre-occupied with ourselves; our needs, our cultural norms, our experiences with sexism, and our worth to the world and to white men and white patriarchal structures. We see ourselves as the center of everything. This means we rarely believe that People of Color's lives are equally valuable or that experiences different from our own are equally valid.

We may claim to not see color to deal with the dissonance of not being able or willing to notice racial differences and simultaneously treat people with respect. Instead, we tell ourselves a lie about only seeing what is on the inside, when what we mean is, "I see you as white." This ultimately means, "I do not have to see you."

What About Me?

It is in this phase that white women tend to call out "reverse racism" and indicate that we are not (but should be!!) entitled to the same supports that People of Color have. For example, we might assert that our children can't get into college or we got passed up for a job because of spots set aside for People of Color. We do this despite the fact that more college seats are reserved for white people, affirmative action has primarily benefitted white women, and reverse racism does not exist in systems designed by and for white people.

Our internal dialogue may be around how hard life is due to sexism (or other oppressions such as classism or homophobia), and it may very well be true that our lives are difficult. What is missing is the willingness to look at the relative hardships of People of Color, especially those who also experience marginalization around other areas of identity such as class or sexual orientation. We may believe People of Color in some way cause our oppression. We further believe any of our experiences of oppression cancel out privilege. When racism is brought up, we view it as an invalidation of our own experience. This is illustrated when white women respond to the Black Lives Matter movement with the statement, "All Lives Matter." We hear "*Only* Black lives matter," as if asserting the value of Black lives takes something from us.

Because sexism is very real, it can be easy to retreat to using the tools of Capitulation when we feel powerless in a given situation. In the workplace, white women may feel stretched between the expectations of the white men in power above us and the unmet needs of the People of Color we supervise or who we purport to serve in our communities.

On rare occasions, we've been called in to provide training or coaching for white women supervisors when People of Color report that these supervisors are treating them badly and not understanding them. Even with extensive coaching, white women in this phase may feel we are the victims of blame, unfairly accused. In Capitulation, we believe the Person of Color is being given more support and rights than we are, based on the sole fact that we are white. If we hold the role of middle manager, we may be keen to share the amount of stress we are under as women and use this to justify why we are tough on our supervisees. What we fail to admit is that we are white women being racist against People of Color who depend on us for their job, and there is an additional power dynamic that requires self-reflection and consideration.

The power dynamics of race still exist when the roles are reversed, and the white woman is the supervisee. Even without positional power in an organization, white women usually still feel entitled to "having my side heard equally," at the expense of

People of Color. White women in Capitulation commonly flip responsibility for our microaggressions—our subtle, unintentional acts of everyday racism—to the Person of Color. By calling it "reverse racism," we can excuse our part in the exchange and blame the Person of Color who got the institutional support we felt we deserved. It is rare that People of Color are supported at all by our institutions in these cases. Yet, a white woman in Capitulation likely believes People of Color are given the benefit of the doubt all the time, which is the opposite of reality. If they are to be believed, People of Color are generally expected to provide indisputable truth of a white woman's *intention* to discriminate, rather than have the impact of the action on them serve as evidence.

For example, a white woman we worked with got upset when her Black coworker complained about her using the racist term *thug*. To justify her use of this word, the white woman asked for support from a Black friend who was not offended by the word and then looked it up in Webster's Dictionary (not the anti-racist word bible one might hope) to rationalize her innocence. This view that her perspective, backed by a book propagated by white men, was superior and canceled out that of her Black colleague, detracted from the larger pattern of her behaviors that went beyond one word. She returned to the dialogue loaded with information to argue why her intention and action were not racist, rather than listen with curiosity and empathy to her coworker's experience.

In Capitulation, a white woman does not consider impact because she is so invested in her intentions. We tend to claim we are the victims when People of Color point out our unconscious bias. This is because our analysis of racism doesn't allow us to see how we can still be "good" people if we are doing something racist, especially when we did not mean to cause harm and have internalized the narrative of our innocence.

Silent Consent

Laura describes how she didn't know about the concept of white privilege until she was twenty-two and came to the White Privilege Conference. She had grown up in an all-white area of Wisconsin, where she had no friends or classmates of color. While she never thought about racism, she remembers from the time she was a little girl, being put in check by her uncles who called her "Mouth." They did this because, "I carried a voice, and my mom wanted me to [speak up for myself]." This part of her personality didn't align with her physical features of being a small, blue-eyed, blonde girl. The positive attention she received for her conventional beauty conflicted with the negative feedback she received for speaking her mind, and she internalized the sexist messages that she was supposed to act the way she looked, meaning demure and acquiescent.

As she became an anti-racist activist, she consciously fought these messages, but she received feedback that she was "a bitch" and not the "safe hire" people had been led to believe. She was told that her employers felt she would be a good person to guide them through white privilege work, but she was a big disappointment when she began directly naming oppressive behaviors and systems (i.e., what they supposedly hired her to do).

Laura's story is common for many white women who are trying to strike a balance between navigating the roles dictated to them from white supremacy and sexism and finding their voices to advocate for justice. The kind of feedback she received is meant to keep white women quiet. We connect this sexist socialization to one reason why white women in Capitulation, unlike Laura, stay silent when racist acts occur.

Tilman exemplified Capitulation when a group she belonged to, named "Solidarity Against the Mikado," protested outside a Seattle production of said play several times. The protesters merely asked the attendees to read a brochure and consider the negative impact that the stereotypical characters played by mostly white men had on people of Asian descent. *The Mikado* patrons, mostly older white people, countered with phrases like, "You just don't understand," or "Nothing is meant by it."

By the third protest, the exchanges became more mean-spirited and colder; the vitriol with which white people responded was telling of their underlying racist assumptions. Even though this was just an amateur production of an antiquated operetta, and the approach was peaceful and respectful, these white patrons acted as if they were defending themselves against an aggressive attack. They did not want to be bothered with a different view and used their privilege to push past the protesters.

Tilman's place at that protest was to be an ally—to use her white privilege to pass out flyers and to dialogue with the patrons. They would often approach her instead of the Asian American protesters because of her race, gender, and age. The protest organizers also knew patrons would be more prone to listen to what Tilman had to say because of their shared whiteness.

But when it most counted, she capitulated. During that third protest, a white man yelled at her protest partner and friend, a Japanese American man, "Well if you don't like it, GO HOME!" Tilman did not actively interrupt him, even knowing that the target of this insult was an American citizen, a veteran, and a survivor of the WWII Japanese American concentration camps.

Instead of telling the white man he was out of line, Tilman used a small voice and tried to cajole him into reason. She could have actively checked him, telling him directly his statement was racist and defending her partner, but she didn't. She allowed herself to empathize way too much with this white man rather than with her friend who was being attacked. Tilman allowed internalized sexism to tell her that she should not confront him; that she should stay in her place and submit.

Even worse, when the protest was over and she was walking back to her car alone because her friend chose to distance himself from her, Tilman rationalized why what happened wasn't fair TO HER! Didn't her friend realize how hard she had tried and how difficult it was to do the right thing in the moment?

It is true that these situations are often uncomfortable for everyone involved and not easy for white women who have been socialized to prioritize the comfort of white people. We aren't practiced in talking about racism, and responses need to happen quickly. But it is important to own when we back down in the face of white male patriarchy and to wrestle with the reasons why, so we can ultimately change our behavior.

Between Helpless and Powerful

Women in Capitulation define racism as bad people doing bad things, such as white supremacists or people who use the n-word. We certainly have nothing in common with jerks like that! Therefore, as good people, we cannot possibly do anything racist. We usually claim we treat everyone the same regardless of differences. Terrie pointed out the heart of white women's thinking in this stage: "Racism is just so sad." Sigh.

If we do witness someone being treated unfairly due to racism, we may claim to feel helpless to do anything in the moment by saying we didn't have the right language, time, resources, or sense of safety to speak up. In addition, because we are "treating everyone fairly," we see no real reason to speak up against racism. Jerks will be jerks and there's nothing we can do about it. Besides, we may say, "That generation will die off soon anyway and you can't change someone's mind when they are set in their ways." This provides a convenient ageist narrative (elderly people can't learn) to justify inaction.

Mallory shared a story of how racism influenced her high school to teach her skills to protect herself as a girl.

In New Orleans, when I was in the ninth grade, they integrated the high school; I'd been going to an all-white high school up until that point. And the week before the other kids were bused into our school, they had an assembly for all the girls, and they taught us how to defend ourselves. And I had these two really strong reactions to it. I was trying to explain to my friends how bad that was, and why it was bad, and not being able to get through to them. I was sputtering I was so angry.

And then the second thing I learned from that was women can defend themselves against men. That changed my brain. I learned the hand movement of twisting out of someone's grasp, and I practiced, and practiced, and practiced, until there wasn't anybody who could keep my hand inside their grip.

While she appreciated that the self-defense course helped her feel more powerful, she recognized that the only reason the school wanted her to have those skills was to defend herself against Black people.

The tension between the perceived lack of safety due to racism and our actual physical safety due to sexism is most apparent in Capitulation. Ilsa frequently shares a story about the time she realized she holds the stereotype that Black men are dangerous when a friend caught her locking the car door as a Black man walked past. Many white women will quickly respond claiming to be afraid of all men. Instead of exploring Ilsa's experience and asking her more about why recognizing this stereotype was important to her, white women react as if implicated by *her story* themselves. Capitulation causes us to redirect the conversation to a universal context of sexism (all men pose a threat), a place in which we can more comfortably discuss our oppression, rather than also seeing the reality of racism. The familiarity of surviving sexism in the face of potential violence trumps any possibility that we might also be perpetuating racism.

We hear white women saying it isn't a "safe space" for conversation when People of Color become animated in their responses to racism. A Person of Color may offer us very tempered feedback and we still read it as aggression, based more on our unexamined stereotypes than on the way the person addressed us. In these situations, we will often quickly shut down or try to find solutions without truly understanding the issues. We may redirect to a more generalized worldview, claiming that everyone faces hardships. We may state that the problems are too big to ever make a change and use this to justify inaction. White women use the common refrain "Let's agree to disagree" to avoid the discomfort we erroneously conflate with safety in race conversations.

If we don't feel the Person of Color is willing to recant or temper their response once we have given the clue that we are feeling threatened, we may decide to contact their supervisor or even the police to re-center our need for "safety." We witnessed this in the video of Amy Cooper, a white woman, confronting Christian

Cooper, a Black man, in Central Park when he asked her to put her dog on a leash. She first responds angrily and approaches him, attempting to exercise her internalized superiority. When he doesn't comply with her demand that he stop recording her with his phone, she calls the police and claims to feel threatened. Rather than fearing for her safety as she claims to the police, she recognizes the power she holds over his actual safety.

Amy Cooper took this action on May 25, 2020, the same day George Floyd was murdered by police officers.

Passive Aggression

In dealing with sexism white women have learned it is often easier to work around a white man than to engage with him directly in what could turn into a power struggle. In this case, avoiding conflict and agreeing to disagree is a strategic move to survive sexism. We may say we agree and nod and smile, then work behind the scenes for a different outcome that allows us more control in the situation. Or we may approach a man in a way that feels complimentary and caring to him in order to make a request, rather than stating our desires directly. We use the tactic of asking questions instead of making demands to allow white men to feel they are the decision makers. Saying, for instance, "Do you think you could wash the dishes tonight?" rather than, "It's your turn to wash the dishes."

The strategy we use with white men of deferring and smiling to get our way is maladaptive when used with People of Color. In Capitulation, we lack an understanding of how race changes who holds power in our relationships. With white men, passive aggression is used to accommodate the relative lack of power we have as women; with People of Color, this strategy is inappropriate because we as white women actually hold institutional power in most situations.

An example of how this can manifest is when white teachers discipline Children of Color in their classrooms, in particular Black boys. Both Ilsa and Tilman have heard stories from Black students who describe being confused when a white teacher is smiling while punishing them. The student might think, "Why is she smiling at me when she is sending me to the office? She must enjoy punishing me."

We've done this ourselves as teachers. The narrative we thought we were communicating was, "I like you, even though I am punishing you." According to the Department of Education Office for Civil Rights, in 2014, Black students represented 16 percent of the student population but 32–42 percent of students suspended or expelled. In preschool, Black children represented 18 percent of enrollment but 48 percent of preschool children receiving more than one out-of-school suspension.[2] The truth we weren't telling ourselves was, "I am overly punishing you because I am uncomfortable with you and feel entitled to be able to control your body." All the while, we believed we can also come across as nice, which is all we need to prop up the narrative of our goodness.

While planning a conference, Ilsa attempted to use a passive-aggressive approach with a multiracial woman. She had heard that this woman, one of the lead conference organizers, had not held any subcommittee meetings. Ilsa approached her and asked how she was doing. She then offered to help if this Woman of Color needed anything. Finally, Ilsa revealed she had heard (the subtext of talking behind the woman's back obvious) that the woman had not been holding meetings. Angrily, this woman responded that Ilsa should ask her what she wanted to know directly, not couch her disapproval in a mask of caring. Although Ilsa did care about the woman, the true purpose of asking after her well-being was to make sure she was doing her job. Thus, Ilsa situated herself as a supervisor, rather than a collaborator, and her supposed caring was disingenuous.

As teachers, smiling made us feel better for removing a child whose body or behavior made us uncomfortable with parts of ourselves we did not want to face. Smiling while punishing a Black child did not help us navigate oppression or work around someone who had power over us. Nor did we have to take account for the harm we caused in the child's life.

In planning the conference, starting with asking how the woman was doing served to help Ilsa feel better about herself and mask the actual purpose of the conversation, which was to make sure the Woman of Color was doing what Ilsa expected. Both of these examples illustrate the passive aggressive, gaslighting nature of Capitulation.

The Politics of Capitulation

Hillary Clinton is an example of a white woman who illustrates the phase we call Capitulation in her political actions. While she is an extraordinarily strong woman, the fact remains that her drive to be elected took a back seat to the essential needs of her husband. She actively supported his campaigns by propagating racist ideology such as the stereotype of Black boys as "super-predators." Only after he'd served his two terms was she allowed to advance her political career with the support of white men. She is as smart if not smarter than Bill Clinton, but she did not have the systemic power to move ahead without first being a First Lady. At that point, she chose to run against a Black man and benefitted from her husband's racist dog whistling during her campaign.

Patriarchy cajoles women to rationalize taking a back seat to the men in their lives while still doing their bidding, with the hope they would eventually be allowed to pursue their dreams as well. Clinton understood that her power was connected to that of her white male husband. Historically, this approach has rarely worked for white women because we give up the power within ourselves. Even when Hillary finally got the democratic nomination, white men and women turned away from her in favor of Donald Trump. Yet the allure remains, and we continue to believe the lie of the promise of white supremacy.

Final Thoughts

Introspection in Capitulation is difficult because any suggestion of white privilege challenges our identity as good, loving people. We often care deeply about the Communities of Color we believe we serve. We've been told we are good caretakers, and, because of the role sexism prescribes for us, taking care of others feels comfortable. Yet, we expect People of Color to continue their historic role of serving as our caretakers, particularly catering to our comfort.

Racism makes us *very sad*, although we don't speak up about it because we've been told to be quiet, that our voices don't matter, and we don't want to lose what little sense of comfort and control we do have. At the same time, we might feel appalled at the idea we've received any benefits from white privilege or respond with anger (usually behind someone's back) when our collusion with racism is pointed out.

Recently, when talking with an African American friend Tilman said, "White privilege may have informed how I created the agenda for our meeting." Without skipping a beat, he replied, "May have informed? DID inform!" His response was absolutely true, and it felt like a jolt. She was so comfortably in Capitulation when she uttered those words that it took her friend's response for her to recognize that, of course, white privilege informed her agenda. Were she not able to access the tools of later phases in this model, she would have responded as if she was personally wounded by his retort.

White women often say, "It is interesting to think about..." in our workshops when reflecting on racism that People of Color experience. This type of voyeuristic relationship exists when white women see ourselves as distinct and separate from POC. Patricia Hill Collins writes, "The privileged become voyeurs, passive onlookers who do not relate to the less powerful, but who are interested in seeing how the 'different' live."[3] We're essentially disconnected from our collective humanity in the stages of Immersion and Capitulation.

Feeling Capitulation

Put one hand on your hip and the other in front of your face to symbolize a mirror. Look at yourself in this mirror and focus on how you feel about yourself. Now move around with this "mirror" in front of you. Don't get distracted by other people in your path, even if you bump into them. Imagine offering an apology to a Person of Color but not meaning it. If you encounter a white man, go in whatever direction he indicates.

- As you held this gesture, what felt natural to you? What felt unnatural?
- What feelings came up for you? Where did these feelings land in your body?
- If you were with other women when you tried this gesture, how did their bodies feel and look to you? How did you feel toward them?

Strategic Questions for Capitulation

- What most worries you about sexism?
- How do you see yourself fighting sexism?
- How do you balance the care you have for white men in your life and your experiences with sexism?
- What most worries you about racism?
- What would it mean to you or how would your life change if you entertained the idea you had received unearned advantages because of your race?
- Talk about the similarities and differences between sexism and racism.

6

Defense

*Because [as white feminists] we were basically
well-meaning individuals, the idea of being part of the
problem of racism (something I had associated with
extremists or institutions but not with myself) was genuinely
shocking to us. And the issue was also terrifying, in the
sense that we constantly felt that at any second we might
err again with respect to racism, that we didn't know the
rules and therefore didn't know how to prevent that from
happening. There was...a way racism was disembodied
from our discussions, sometimes an issue of standpoint,
sometimes one of etiquette, and definitely an issue
that provoked the intense frustration that came of
not being able to "get it" or to "get it right."*

— Ruth Frankenberg

WHILE CAPITULATION is passive, Defense strategies are more active. For example, in Capitulation we might respond to an accusation of racism with, "I'm sorry you feel that way," and a paternalistic smile. In Defense, we'd say, "Never in my life have I been disrespected in this way!" The "I" we defend is the "nice" and "good" person who could not have caused harm to another person intentionally but also who has learned not to see People of Color as a fully deserving of respect—or even fully human.

White women in the stage we call Defense develop a heightened awareness of how we've been harmed by personal and institutional sexism. We build bonds and movements with other white women in our shared struggles against patriarchy.

As we move into Defense, white women also awaken to the reality of racism. But, as Frankenberg points out, we're not really sure how or what to do and may lash out in our frustration. Because we are actively fighting the weight of sexist oppression, we frequently find it difficult to acknowledge any unearned advantages from white privilege. To admit we behave in racist ways, make racist assumptions (even unconsciously), or benefit from white privilege feels like it would undermine all of our hard work as women. Instead, we vehemently defend our behaviors when we are called on our racism. After all, we are strong, powerful women who have battled extremely hard to get ahead. Don't you see that?!

Defense Reversal

Some white women connect more with men than women and, therefore, do not identify with a phase of development where a "sisterhood" or affinity with other women who also battle sexism is a strong component. There may even be a reversal, where they'd rather not spend any time with women. Shelly spoke to this in her life:

> As a young female, totally hetero-normatively raised, [I] really felt very comfortable with men all of my life, more so than women, possibly because of the cattiness. And because of the power my father gave me to, "Just be who you are and stand up and don't take any guff from anybody else."
>
> I got challenged to go back and try to create relationships with women. And then I did, but...I don't show up thinking, and behaving, and being like what they wanted me to. I feel like this was more like the new age-y feminist circle...I didn't feel like I fit in there either. So, I'm going to go hang out with men again because I don't get beat up there. I get to be me when I'm with men.

In Shelly's example, women are stereotyped as "catty" and lacking individual power to stand up for themselves. It is not until she is challenged by men to build relationships with women that she agrees to try this. She then has an experience of not connecting with a group of feminists and quickly goes back to spending time mostly with men. She's not denying the existence of institutional sexism but doesn't see it impacting her life in a way where she feels she would need to address this with other women.

We've encountered this with white women working in male-dominated fields as well. Some don't have any desire to bond with other women but still demonstrate most of the other characteristics of Defense. Independent and forceful, these women actively resist any implication that their success has come from a modicum of white privilege. They see themselves as strong women who have overcome obstacles weaker women would get hung up on. They don't need other women; they can handle these dudes on their own.

Fighting for Crumbs: Sexism Versus Racism

White women activists in the Defense stage often believe we have to choose between fighting against patriarchy or racism (we don't have time for both!), without recognizing how these struggles are connected. Because sexism is so obvious to us, we may think the needs of women must trump all other causes. We don't believe a victory for People of Color would necessarily be a victory for us, and we fail to acknowledge that any women's movement that doesn't address racism leaves out Women of Color. This dichotomous thinking on the part of white women, and our unwillingness to see how our best interests are attached to the interests of People of Color, is a demonstration of our deeply ingrained internalized racial superiority.

Johanna described this reaction succinctly when she shared the following experience:

It actually harkens to the White Privilege Conference, in one of my earlier years of going there. There was a panel of Black men, and after that there was a panel of Black women. The Black women made an assertion that Black men would be better off partnering with Black women because of the way that Black women can understand their experiences with whiteness. It just pissed me off.

I don't know if there's a sexism piece in there, but there may be an internalized sexism piece…I was like "Righteous White Person." I know there's no such thing as reverse racism, but I wonder what sexism was triggered. I was being left out of the equation, and I hadn't ever had People of Color on a stage telling me where I didn't belong. It went against my rules of equality. Why are you putting one group down when we are trying to get at racial justice? Why am I so hated?

Johanna continued to reflect on how feeling excluded in that moment allowed her to rationalize her racism:

With the Black women, we are supposed to be on the same page, but now they were saying I'm part of the problem… One of the things that helped soothe me, when I came home, was keeping sexism and racism separate. I could watch Men of Color being sexist, and that would somehow soothe my shame over my racism. "Yeah, so you are going to side with men, when they are the problem? I see who you choose." Because it's personal…

White privilege can allow white women to think that "sisterhood" transcends race. When a Woman of Color contradicts this ideology by making it clear we are NOT all sisters who experience sexism in the same way, white women, like Johanna, may become defensive and angry. We bring the conversation back to sexism, a place where we're more comfortable, as she did in paying special attention to the ways Men of Color act this out. They are now an easier target than white men for our feeling excluded. We might make up a narrative that Women of Color who are more connected to Men of Color are acting out of their internalized sexism and not taking care of themselves. In reality, we are just feeling left out. Our internalized white superiority tells us that we should be in the center of everything, never incidental, and our internalized sexism tells us we are innocent of any accusations of racism.

As Johanna wrapped up her memory of that panel, she shared her thinking, "I was like, if WPC wants me to keep coming back, they need to stop doing that in-group stuff. There's no room for me." She assumed the conference should be organized around her, as that was her white experience to that point. Taking personally a broader statement about racism and wondering, "Why am *I* so hated?" most commonly shows up in Defense. There was no acknowledgment at that time that she and other white women were not the primary concern for the Women of Color on the panel.

Our involvement with activism tenuously hangs on people doing activism in the way we think it should be done. We have seen many white women say they cannot support the Black Lives Matter movement when some people are destroying property. Friends on social media share, "I used to be a supporter until…" Believing we get to dictate how activism happens and then saying we don't support an entire movement, that we no longer believe Black lives matter, illustrates one of the many ways white superiority shows up in the Defense stage.

Dena also spoke about the failure of white women to see intersections of different areas of oppression. She said,

> [My] experience is mostly in social justice conferences, in the places that you'd think that people would get the intersection, but oftentimes they don't. I mean real simple experiences seeing white women talking about sexism only and ignoring their whiteness. Seeing that not only in conferences but in organizations where they feel like they are fighting the good fight in terms of those isms and just don't see the intersectionality at all…
>
> I've seen this even more so with white Jewish women. Just the idea that you have a monopoly on pain or oppression

or something like that. It's painful as a white Jewish woman myself. It's really painful. It's very difficult to watch.

This is not to say that anti-Semitism isn't real or needing full attention, especially in our efforts to understand how white supremacy often has anti-Semitic roots. We've also witnessed this with queer white women who ignore whiteness in advocating for gay rights and disabled white women who don't account for the multiple marginalizations of racism and ableism. The more areas where we're experiencing oppression, the more difficult it may be to acknowledge our privilege because we already have to fight for crumbs. Focusing on our self-interests makes sense when our oppression feels ever present. White patriarchy has intentionally aimed to divide us from People of Color, hoping we'll feel we have to choose to align with whiteness to overcome other areas of oppression.

However, white women in the phase of Defense don't see it this way. Should someone suggest we need to address our racism, we often respond with an almost ferocious rationalization of why we put our issues before those of People of Color. To avoid shame, white women will claim to be working on behalf of "all women," even when it is clear we are not.

As the United States feminist movement matured and got traction in the 1970s, it demonstrated the characteristics of the Defense stage. Failing to represent the needs of Women of Color was a willful act, but when the leadership was called out on promoting primarily white women's feminism, they claimed they had no choice. They stopped supporting Shirley Chisolm's campaign on the false promise that white men would take up their platform at the Democratic Convention. They erroneously believed that in the long run their work would be able to help others, once they had won their own privileges and rights.

By neglecting to address racism, the search for gender equality ends up defaulting to the needs of white women. A recent example of this is Gloria Steinem's explanation of why she supported Hillary Clinton over Barack Obama in the 2008 election. In her book, *My Life on the Road* she wrote,

I knew that outside the women's movement, I would be better liked if I chose Obama. Women are always better liked if we sacrifice ourselves for something bigger—and something bigger always means including men, even though something bigger for men doesn't usually mean including women. In choosing Hillary, I would be seen as selfish for supporting a woman "like" me. But that was a warning, too. Needing approval is a female cultural disease, and often a sign of doing the wrong thing…Because I still believed it was too soon for Hillary or any woman to be accepted as commander in chief, I wrote: *If I were Obama, I would not feel personally betrayed by lack of support from someone like me, a new ally. If I were Hillary Clinton, I might feel betrayed by a longtime supporter who left me for a new face.* In other words: Obama didn't need me to win. Hillary Clinton might need me to lose.[1]

Framing her rationale as one of not caving to the desire to be liked or approved confuses the interpersonal with an analysis of institutional racism. By saying that Obama had more of a chance to win the 2008 election because he was a man ignores the reality that he is a Black man who ultimately had less access to institutional power than Hillary. In 1972, Steinem chose to endorse a white man, George McGovern, over a Black woman, Shirley Chisolm, for the Democratic nomination for president. Her rationale changed to justify aligning with whiteness each time.

Steinem received feedback from People of Color that she "was asking people to take sexism more seriously than racism." When she was publicly rebuked by a woman she only described as an African American academic, Steinem reacted by saying defensively, "I refuse to be divided on this." Instead of responding with openness and curiosity, Steinem looked for validation from friends of color and wrote a list to rationalize her stance.[2]

We don't fault her decision to support Hillary. It was the framing of sexism without an accounting of racism, coupled with her response to critique, that we see as characteristic of what we call the Defense stage.

This kind of thinking is rooted in historical models where white women rationalize standing up for our civil rights over those of People of Color. There is a pattern of white women signing up to advocate for the rights of People of Color, such as abolition in the 1800s, Civil Rights in the 1960s, Affirmative Action in the late 1970s, and the current Black Lives Matter movement, and then pivoting at critical moments toward our needs and desires for institutional access. In theory, white women seem to understand the idea of "No Separate Peace," the concept that my liberation is inextricably connected to others' liberation, but once we are called upon to change our behavior and to share power, or to directly confront white patriarchy, we have regularly chosen to protect our own privilege as well as the perceived needs of white men. Historically, we have done this even after accepting support and allyship from People of Color, rationalizing that white women deserve to be given equal rights before Men of Color.

As Angela Davis recounts in her book, *Women, Race, and Class*, white women of all classes were actively drawn to the abolitionist movement for several reasons: a sense of camaraderie around experiences of oppression, an opportunity to emerge as organizers and agitators during a time when women had few such chances, and an awareness that abolition could be connected to women's rights.

Davis points out, "As they worked within the abolitionist movement, White women learned about the nature of human oppression—and in the process, also learned important lessons about their own subjugation. In asserting their right to oppose slavery, they protested—sometimes overtly, sometimes implicitly—their own exclusion from the political arena." Through their experiences with the abolition movement, white women learned many skills, such as fundraising, public speaking, and organizing that would ultimately support their fight for gender equality.[3]

In the 1830s, when Sarah and Angelina Grimke, two of the most famous female abolitionists, began to speak out publicly in support of ending slavery, they were met with vengeful attacks by white men and some white women, especially Christians who were incensed by their audacity to defy feminine roles and "challenge God's will."[4]

These experiences led them to more deeply connect the need for women's rights to anti-slavery. They understood that women could not be effective orators and organizers on behalf of enslaved individuals when they were silenced. Unlike Clinton and Steinem, the Grimke sisters never lost their understanding of the connection between women's rights and ending slavery. They insisted that, "women could never achieve their freedom independently of Black people."

> Because the Grimke sisters had such a profound consciousness of the inseparability of the fight for Black Liberation and the fight for Women's Liberation, they were never caught in the ideological snare of insisting that one struggle was absolutely more important than the other. They recognized the dialectical character of the relationship between the two causes.[5]

However, while the Grimke sisters understood the connected nature of these two causes, White women who followed in their footsteps were not as devoted to this idea.

Lucretia Mott and Elizabeth Cady Stanton, both well-known abolitionists, experienced sexism when they were barred from actively participating in the 1840 World Anti-Slavery Convention. Unlike the Grimke sisters, this exclusion caused Mott and Cady Stanton to redirect their efforts to women's rights, actions we identify as emblematic of the Defense phase. They organized what is considered to be the first women's rights convention in the United States, the Seneca Falls Convention. During this conference, men were invited to share their thoughts on the resolutions, and Frederick Douglass was among them.

While most resolutions were passed by all, women and men alike, there was great resistance to the radical resolution to allow women to vote. After much debate, with Frederick Douglass using his male status to stand by Stanton, this resolution passed. This demonstrated the strength in combining forces against white male supremacy.[6]

However, significant groups were missing from the Seneca Falls Convention. Working-class women for one and Black women for another. The Grimke sisters had chastised several female anti-slavery societies for ignoring the conditions of Black women and for blatantly racist sentiments, especially because of the important contributions that Black women had made toward the fight for women's suffrage. Under the leadership of Mott and Stanton middle- and upper-class white women continued the trend of jostling to center their needs in the fight for equality.

During this time, Frederick Douglass's daughter, while granted admission to a girl's seminary in New York, was banned from attending classes with the white girls. The school principal was a proclaimed abolitionist woman, who demonstrated Defense when she refused to back down.[7] Despite Douglass's willingness to support women's suffrage, he frequently did not receive white women's support in fighting racist practices.

For all white women who are sick of facing sexism every day and living with its consequences, fighting for our rights is necessary. In Defense though, we are focused on the idea that patriarchy is the greatest block to equality everywhere. We do not consider there may be other oppressions as great as, or greater than, our own. We don't acknowledge the important intersections of race and gender that complicate rather than invalidate our experiences. When we are called out on a narrow view of white women's liberation, we often use the same strategies we learned to combat sexism, including intellectualizing, rationalizing, passively or directly aggressing, and claiming authority to fend off criticism.

I Got This

Another pattern of Defense is to approach people in a way that is quick, direct, and "right." To deal with sexism, we may believe we must "lean in," as Sheryl Sandberg encourages, make sure our voice gets heard, and be more forceful than white men to convince people of the value of our ideas. Peggy described Sandberg's work: "She's about getting women to do what men used to do."

As a result, many white women identify as perfectionists. Shelly shared:

> Many of the white women friends that I have, we have noticed in ourselves an extreme need to be perfect. Needing to do it all right, needing to never show a flaw and the idea is that if I am not perfect then I am not lovable. If you can see that I didn't do that thing right, then I am nothing.

Whiteness has fooled us into believing perfection is possible, and sexism dictates we can't mess up. We know that one visible mistake may remind white men we don't deserve to be in this workplace or deserve to be loved, resulting in a loss of access to privilege through our relationships with them. Therefore, it is difficult for us to be vulnerable or admit when we don't understand something unless we are asking a man to help us with fixing our car or a computer problem. In the Defense stage, we can become rigid and stubborn, unwilling to consider others' points of view.

It often causes problems for People of Color when we exhibit these behaviors in multicultural settings. We talk more than anyone else in the room. We bring in agendas packed with ideas that we pretty much already want to do and don't leave time for debate or conversation, though we feign ignorance or become exasperated when this is pointed out to us. We regularly sum up what People of Color have contributed and claim it as our own. Should an issue around race arise, we may pretend to fully understand already, claim we don't have time to discuss it, become impatient, or put it off to an unforeseen and likely nonexistent time in the future.

Tilman and Ilsa demonstrated the power hoarding commonly found in Defense when planning the national conference we mentioned in the introduction to this book. Throughout the planning year, there were moments when committee members came and went for various life reasons, though we saw all members as vital to the sustenance of the group—at first. Everyone in the group took the lead on one aspect of planning, such as fundraising, community outreach, organizing a special event at the conference, etc., with the idea that each of us brought equal value to the collective planning effort. Slowly, Ilsa and Tilman started to take over the lead of every part. A concern would be raised and we convinced ourselves we were the only ones capable enough to tackle any issues in any area.

The regular facilitation and planning of the local meetings with twenty or more volunteers tended to be stewarded by four or so people, and Tilman and Ilsa firmly planted ourselves as two of those stewards. Ilsa volunteered to send all of the emails to volunteers. By doing this, she positioned herself in control of all of the important communication about the conference. She also benefited by having her name consistently associated with the conference, a subtle form of advertising as she was building her consulting business.

Some tensions occurred during meetings and retreats when some of the Women of Color voiced that Tilman and Ilsa were micromanaging the agendas and processes. We were doing just that. We rationalized this behavior by telling ourselves that we were following the conference founder's, a Black man's, leadership by doing what was needed to move things forward. We had very little curiosity about how our white superiority was showing up and quickly dismissed concerns by stressing the lack of time to do all the planning. We would regularly meet to talk with another white woman about the challenges we faced, without circling back to the People of Color on the team. What we called "caucusing" was, in reality, gossiping. It wasn't until years later that we recognized and admitted the many ways we undermined the conference planning and, worse yet, our relationships with other local activists.

Tilman shared another story of pushing through her agenda in the workplace.

An example of this happened at work not too long ago, when I was in a meeting with mostly white women and one Black woman. We were tackling a difficult situation that had heavy financial implications, and I determined this to be time sensitive. I was anxious and uncomfortable to begin with and was using all of my "super brain power" to get the job done! I created a sense of urgency and wanted to solve the situation as soon as possible. We were moving forward at a clip that was comfortable for me, except that the Black woman, who is my elder, colleague, and friend, kept putting up what I considered to be roadblocks. I became frustrated and impatient. Instead of stopping to ask why she was doing this and considering that she might have a good reason for trying to slow us down, my voice became louder and my remarks became more sharply directed at her. While this strategy resulted in moving toward what I deemed a reasonable solution in a small amount of time, it also resulted in my colleague physically recoiling from me.

Here was that moment when I could have felt curious about what was going on for her. On the contrary, over the next few days, I tried relentlessly to rationalize my behavior in my mind with a blend of defensiveness and righteousness to keep my sense of comfort with how I'd behaved.

But it stuck with me, so I talked to my colleague. She described my face at that moment as becoming contorted, so much so that she barely recognized me. Her recoiling from me was a recognition of the speed with which my white superiority trumped all else. I didn't like having to recognize the ugliness in me that caused my colleague and friend to see me as a contorted person, and I didn't want to feel the discomfort of knowing I hurt her. But the fact is, I did disrespect and hurt her, and it was my duty to acknowledge this and try to do better the next time. Had I stayed defensive, I never would have checked in with her or believed her feedback about me.

This small moment illustrates a bigger trend with white women in Defense. People of Color regularly identify a pattern where white women push our agendas through and assume we know best what will work for a group. We claim not to have the time to get input from the communities most impacted by our decisions.

In the nonprofit sector, a white male-controlled system of grants reinforces our behavior with monetary rewards for meeting arbitrary deadlines. To provide services to Communities of Color, white women often end up competing against one another for the necessary funds. We tend to believe we know better what white men are looking for in grant applications and may rush through the process without taking time for any relationship with the people we say we're intending to serve with the money. The majority of nonprofits say they value authentic relationships with Communities of Color. However, most actually work from a service model where true engagement, much less accountability to Communities of Color, is seen as ancillary at best to everyday operations. White women benefit from holding prestigious roles in these organizations due to our ability and willingness to meet the needs of white men who give us access to the resources that pay our salaries.

Take What I Want and Leave the Rest

Many white women appropriate Indigenous culture, looks, and spiritual practices. This may be because we've given up our own ethnic roots in trying to gain the spoils of whiteness and now aren't connected to our cultural practices. We may believe our culture lacks spiritual depth, or we want to identify with the mythologized images we hold of Indigenous Peoples. We may believe Indigenous cultures better honor our feminine side, as we connect with Mother Earth and seek out more matriarchal societies in efforts to counter sexism.

Cultural appropriation is based on stereotypes of Indigenous Peoples and is usually done without regard to colonization, historic genocide, or current struggles faced by Indigenous communities. Dr. Adrienne Keene has been writing extensively about this for years on her blog, *Native Appropriations.* In her article "But Why Can't I Wear a Hipster Headress?" she says, "By the sheer fact that you live in the United States you are benefiting from the history of genocide and continued colonialism of Native peoples. That land you're standing on? Indian land. Taken illegally so your ancestor who came to the US could buy it and live off it, gaining valuable capital (both monetary and cultural) that passed down through the generations to you... [B]y dismissing and minimizing the continued subordination and oppression of Natives in the US by donning your headress, you are contributing to the culture of power that continues the cycle today."[8]

With a new understanding of systems of oppression, particularly patriarchy, it is not uncommon for white women to want to dissociate ourselves from those systems. Still seeing our *individual* identity as the primary concern, we may engage in cultural appropriation to try to distance from our whiteness. By being visibly different from "the man," we believe we no longer carry the burden of the oppressor and, therefore, maintain our identity as "good" people. If I just don't look like a corporate white person, that's enough to fight racism, right?

Ilsa shares why she engaged in cultural appropriation.

> As I sought ways to distance myself from whiteness and heteropatriarchy, I traveled with only women, wore a medicine bag, learned to spit, and worked in the campus Women's Center. I saw many Women of Color as exotic and desirable. I wanted them to be my friends and lovers, as they then symbolized the non-racist, anti-patriarchy identity I sought. These relationships, based on objectification for the purpose of boosting my image, were always short lived.

In a white woman's mind, cultural appropriation can also manifest as a desire to connect with People of Color. We refer to ourselves negatively as vanilla or white bread and seek "flavor" from People of Color. We think and say, "I love your people so much. You have so much culture that I don't have." There is a deep swell of wanting to show how much we have in common with People of Color, which is tied to defensiveness about our collusion with white privilege. We think if we are seen as more similar to POC, even if by appropriating artifacts and cultural practices, we can't possibly be racist.

Katy shared an experience to illustrate this: "I have multiple items of jewelry that I don't wear anymore. A Buddha necklace and I loved it. Then, holy crap, when someone who knew about it and I didn't. I was embarrassed, more out of my ignorance. I didn't understand the history of this image—and felt trampled on."

This response wasn't one of curiosity or understanding; it was defensive. Her word choice of feeling embarrassed and trampled on (we talk more about feedback framed as violence in the chapter on white women's tears) led her to just put the jewelry to the side, not to investigate what she owned and why she owned it. These "out of sight, out of mind" responses may lead white women to feel more comfortable with the mistakes we have made, but they don't add to our bank of understanding or our fully engaging with People of Color. We quickly say, "I'm so sorry! I'm so sorry!" while having no idea what we're apologizing for.

Cultural appropriation is also a way some white women try to break out of the confines of the "good girl" box of sexism. Ilsa's story illustrates this.

> I never wanted to be called a "lady," which I regarded as a code for wealthy, nice, good, proper, white girl and, therefore, limiting to my full expression and not fitting with my working-class upbringing. As Blackness is stereotyped as the antithesis of those qualities, I latched on to that identity to defy sexism and deny my white privilege. When I was twelve years old, I learned all of the lyrics to 2-Live Crew songs at the height of the controversy over putting parental advisories on music. Ironically, the song I knew best, "We Want Some Pussy," is completely sexist, which is also what made it so BAD and, therefore, so appealing.

Mylie Cyrus, a white female music artist, is famous for doing the same thing. As she tried to shake off her good girl Hannah Montana image, she put in gold teeth, learned to twerk (arguably), and used Black people as props in her videos and performances. This shortcut to a "gritty" image is one strategy white women use to make us feel more grown up and consequential. It gives us a false sense of community with People of Color that is based on taking from them whatever we want to craft our new image. We're essentially telling the world, "Look at me! I'm not nice, I'm Black." How convenient that we can do this without genuinely sacrificing any of our privilege and often making money off of this edgy identity.

The outcomes for these white women who put on a temporary mask of "Blackness" contrasts sharply with what Alicia Garza, one of the founders of the Black Lives Matter movement, identifies for Black people. "This too was an impact of the War on Drugs: a fetishization of Black culture as outlaw, as rebel, as renegade, while criminalizing Black people whether we were outlaw, rebel, renegade, or not." She connects this with overpolicing of Black communities and mass incarceration.[9]

White women may defensively claim, "Well, everything comes from some culture. Should I just not wear jewelry or listen to music I like?!" This serves to situate the problem with the Person of Color, who is clearly "too sensitive," rather than taking a deeper look at why we want to engage in cultural appropriation and the harmful impact of reducing complex cultures to objects and artifacts.

I Love Your People

Another form of appropriation is more subtle. White women in the stage of Defense may want to appear closer to People of Color with the choices we make (often in awkward ways). Johanna illustrated this with a story about a short exchange, "We were just with some friends, and one of them was African American, and she asked what we wanted to listen to. My wife said, 'Nina Simone.'

Is that what we normally listen to? (Pause) I don't know when I'll get out of that—seeking the approval of People of Color."

This example demonstrates how quickly our minds and responses are keyed up to try to connect with People of Color even when we aren't being authentic. Johanna went on to explain how she could easily recognize a parallel example when people were trying to connect with her as a queer woman:

> I try to say "Hi" to People of Color in white spaces. I'll just say, "Hi." I'm not sure if they are on to me. I know where I'm coming from but I'm not sure of the impact. [However, I can see the impact] when my wife, Jill, and I are walking around and we are holding hands. We see people wanting to acknowledge us [and let us know they are] not homophobes. We think it's cute. We're on to straight folks doing it—so cute. They have such big smiles.

Terrie spoke about the particular way she centered an affirmation of her identity in relationships with People of Color.

> I found a lot of ways to identify with People of Color through class and culture—feeling camaraderie around region, or language, or music, or lived experience as coming from a Jewish family, or being working class, or having a dad who never graduated from high school. I don't remember ever feeling that way about white men, exactly in the same way. What we did have in common was white privilege...
>
> I knew there was sexism, and I knew that there was privilege. But now I'm thinking about how resistant I was to being different from People of Color and it got in the way of my seeing them. Because I was so busy seeing myself in relationship to them, I didn't pay attention to their lived experience when I met them. I was so busy trying to find something that would connect us together and not make us different...It was a little bit of an obsession. But I think it was the resistance to recognizing all the privilege that

I have, that they don't have. I certainly know more about different communities and their cultural experiences now than I did 20 years ago. I think I was resistant, although I didn't think of it as resistant [at the time].

In her mind, Terrie was trying to make a connection. White women in Defense do this by minimizing any difference between ourselves and the People of Color in our lives and, in many ways, interacting with them as if they are stereotypes rather than people. We are not connecting around our similarities in authentic relationships but attempting to prove to ourselves and the world that we are not racist. We're different from other white people because of our appreciation, tolerance, and proximity to People of Color.

We are likely to believe our experiences with sexism mean we fully understand racism, then use this as a tool to try to connect and minimize our differences. White author Julie Landsman writes about this:

> Many white women feel they automatically understand the power of racism simply because as females, they experience sexism. This prevents them from understanding racism in all its institutional and societal—as well as historical— power. When their Black sisters confront them with their own different lives as women because of racism, white women are surprised. It took some very frank and painful conversations for me to stop equating my experience with sexism with my friends' and colleagues' experiences with racism. White women do well when they listen.[10]

That's Not What I Meant!

Characteristics of Defense are likely to show up when we've done something racist and a Person of Color points it out. In 2013, artist Ani DiFranco, well known for her feminism, scheduled a music retreat on a plantation. She was publicly criticized for selecting this location. Her response demonstrates the way she tried to protect her identity as a social activist who cares and shifted the blame to the People of Color who called her out.

Later, when I found out it was to be held at a resort on a former plantation, I thought to myself, "whoa," but I did not imagine or understand that the setting of a plantation would trigger such collective outrage or result in so much high-velocity bitterness...I cancel the retreat now because I wish to restore peace and respectful discourse between people as quickly as possible.[11]

By insisting on "respectful discourse," white women try to dictate the ways in which People of Color are allowed to give us feedback, sometimes referred to as tone policing. DiFranco also sees herself as central in restoring peace rather than the possibility of being instrumental in speaking out against racism.

Because she didn't think about race in her decision, she believed people should not respond so strongly. From birth, most white women are taught a one-sided history that intentionally fails to educate us about racism. However, the defensive reaction of "Well, I didn't know" closes the door to further learning. We don't say, "I didn't know. That's something I should be aware of and learn more about." We say, "I didn't know. Leave me alone," or even, "I didn't know, so, therefore, it must not be true (because otherwise I would have known)."

Katy shared a different manifestation of this dynamic from when she was in high school:

I grew up near McChord Air Force Base, and in my high school they had clubs: Hispanic, Pacific Islander, African American clubs—they had three to four clubs. I was outraged there wasn't a Euro-American club.

[There was a] feeling...of a lot of competition between women—you don't go near my man. Specific Girls of Color [made it] very clear—you had to be careful how you looked at their men—you didn't date their men. Scarcity, born out of competition, or whatever. I can totally understand that sense of outrage. I'm not even fighting for that thing. But why are we fighting over this? That anger—that

I had done something wrong and taken from them, when I hadn't done it! I didn't own slaves! Why did you blame me? [I remember] very specifically being in tears because, "I don't know why so and so was so angry with me." I didn't understand. I felt personally hated. I didn't know why. I'm looking at our interactions. I had no sense of history and privilege. No understanding of my role.

Again, we tend to personalize anger and frustration about racism, then use arguments to assert our lack of individual culpability. Depending on their identity development, the People of Color who were angry with Katy might also be coming from a place where it was easier to target her than to target systemic racism. This caused much pain to everyone involved. Our schools do all young people a disservice when they fail to teach us to think systemically and work collectively. However, even when individually blamed, White women don't have to respond defensively in the way Katy did. We have other options that we'll explore in later stages.

In Katy's example, she believed she understood something about racism that the People of Color in her school failed to recognize; she believed they would not be mad at her if they only understood she didn't own slaves. The tendency to interpret People of Color's experiences through our lens, then feel entitled to weigh in on the validity of those experiences, shows up in all of the first three stages. These are the "Are you sure that was about race?" conversations that are meant to reaffirm white women's goodness and return us to a sense of equilibrium and comfort. In a racist and sexist society, the protection of white women's comfort is paramount, and we internalize both our need for protection (sexism) and entitlement to comfort (white privilege).

Helpful and Nice Aggression

Ilsa talked with a white woman on the phone recently about challenges her equity team was facing. Part of the problem the white woman named was the way people were treating each other in their group. According to her, this is a group where they were all supposed to have the common goal of greater inclusivity and feel safe talking about these issues.

During an equity team meeting, something the white woman had done (she declined to share what exactly it was) had led to an African American man becoming very upset with her. He was yelling, and she said, "I felt threatened. I thought he might literally jump across the table at me." She was upset and felt his behavior—how angry and loud he was—was inappropriate for the group. She was wondering about even continuing to work in the group and thinking about quitting.

But she thought it over and considered what might be going on that would make him that upset. He was a Black man working in a predominantly white organization. He was also a disabled veteran who used a wheelchair. While this didn't mean he wasn't capable of approaching her aggressively, the idea that he had more power than she did in that moment, or posed a physical threat, had more to do with her stereotypes than with reality.

Black male friends have told us about similar situations, where they're speaking to a white woman they disagree with and later she tells their supervisor they were being intimidating and scary. Usually, this comes back to the Black men as a warning about their "aggressive" behavior and can result in their getting fired.

In this situation, not only had the white woman situated herself as the "victim of the dangerous Black man who might jump across the table" but then she also got to see herself as sympathetic and understanding. By taking the time to consider what his experiences with racism might be, she could still see herself as kind and helpful. She did not have to take responsibility for her words and actions that contributed to the outrage in the first place, or her fear response based on, and justified by, her stereotypes. This is another way white women can show up in the stage we call Defense, as the innocent, helpful people who prioritize our comfort at the expense of People of Color's pain.

Please Join, as Long as You Make Me Feel Good

We're pleased to have People of Color join our organization or committee, as long as they don't try to share power. The minute they do, white women in Defense may claim an organization's diversity, equity, and inclusion work is creating a hostile work environment (for white people goes unsaid).

We've seen multiple organization leaders who are mostly white change their email policies, shut down the chat in virtual settings, or ask for people to be fired after social justice advocates started naming racism in the organization. They may ask for so-called civil discourse or lament how everyone used to be so nice to each other. The claim that naming racism divides us, reinforces get-in-line and assimilation messages to People of Color and their allies. More specifically, this is one of the ways punitive anti-Blackness commonly shows up in organizations.

Tilman recounted a relationship she had with an African American male colleague who was known to be thoughtful, smart, and a good critical thinker. At the beginning of their professional relationship, they got along well and talked often about issues of racism and white privilege. With time, when it appeared that he wasn't performing to the job standards set by their agency, he became less accessible to Tilman. Instead of trying to imagine what was going on for her coworker or having a direct conversation with him, Tilman began to resent his relative distance and coldness.

She started to confuse her desire to be seen as an advocate for him with how she was behaving toward him. She wasn't supporting him. She was "innocently" colluding with his supervisor to point out his foibles. She did this because she perceived that his lack of communication with her was somehow connected to his job performance when the two were doubtlessly unrelated. When she didn't get the kind of relationship she had come to expect from him, Tilman threw in the towel and not only stopped trying to be his ally, she allowed others to decide that he wasn't a good fit for the agency and let him go without interfering.

If we go back to the assertion that white women try to soothe the impact of sexism from white men by getting affirmation from People of Color, then when we get feedback from People of Color that we are not needed, our internalized white superiority rises. We move into "Oh yeah! Someone's gonna pay! Look at all I've done for you!" We're likely not acknowledging that our pain is with sexism. Instead, we may turn it around and make the People of Color, whom we perceive as rejecting us, pay the price for our marginalization.

This desire for retribution for perceived harm connects to the historical relationship between white women and Black men discussed previously. We have been used as the reason for white men to kill Black men, and we have a history of actively employing white male authority on our behalf and/or passively accepting this violence in our names. We have internalized that we are good and virtuous, so the fact that both Tilman and the woman Ilsa spoke to saw themselves as victims of their Black colleagues is a result of what we have learned from the intersection of sexism and racism. In Defense, we aren't likely to be empathetic to how People of Color feel and the role our white privilege played; we're bolstering our sense of superiority by focusing on how grateful they should feel to even be invited to be a part of this organization.

Physically Defending Ourselves

Like the training Mallory received at her school, many white women learn self-defense to keep ourselves physically safe. Ilana shared a story of complicated race and gender dynamics where her instincts for safety kicked in.

> I'm going into the room and there is this kind of rowdy energy. At one point, my roommate of color and another person who doesn't live with us were just kind of play fighting, and I get hurt in the process. I was a bystander, and I was trying to walk around the situation, and [the Man of Color] grabs my leg forcing me to face-plant into the kitchen floor.
>
> And so, I don't think. Granted he's drunk. He grabs my

leg and I face-plant. And in an act of just immediate defensiveness, I got up and kicked him in the chest. I self-protect because I was in a fight mode in my house. Most other spaces, I would have just run away and gone to safety. But that was supposed to be my safety. And it was not a head moment, it was a reaction. It was like a gut response. My Mom trained me as a female to be tough...

He didn't realize he had hurt me. He just thought out of the blue I came over and assaulted him...He was in this level sort of roughhousing energy with his friends. But I didn't consent to that. I was sober, and I was just coming home and just trying to get by. And he was really mad. He started yelling and started saying really verbally assaultive things.

I do not regret how I responded only because I know that that instinct might save my life one day as a woman. As a woman, I know the instinct to protect myself physically when my physical space is compromised or threatened, I know that gut could save my life one day.

So, I struggle with that, because I didn't want to hurt him, like, I really didn't. We were friends before this... I have a lot of regrets around my lack of initiation beforehand, and also my awareness of how the microaggressions of the male-dominated space was in my body stronger than I was really aware of it. Because if I reacted that way, then there had to have been more going on for me than I was really willing to admit. So, I have regrets around what I could have done before that moment but in that exact moment, I don't have that regret [of protecting myself].

She recognizes that more was going on for her than just the interaction in the moment. Living in a world where we're experiencing daily small acts of sexism, this might build up in white women if we don't have a healthy way to acknowledge and process what is in our bodies. At the same time, racist messages also build daily in our subconscious and rarely get processed. When under stress, we may lash out at someone who has less systemic power. This could be a physical reaction, as in Ilana's story, but it is more often a verbal dressing down of a Person of Color.

But I'm a Good Anti-Racist: Defensiveness Toward People of Color

As we move into the next stage of identity development, the one we call Projection, we are still so reliant on the outside affirmation of our identities that we can easily revert to the toolset of Defense when called out publicly for our racist behaviors. We may shut down, become stony in response, and then triangulate in private, finding people who agree with us to reaffirm ourselves rather than talking with the person who is upset with us.

Ilsa shared another story from debriefing with the conference planning team where she reverted to her Defense skills after more than fifteen years of actively organizing against racism.

> I was in the large, multiracial group that had been meeting together for several months. A Woman of Color came to the meeting upset about the white dominance in the group process and particularly upset with me. She was palpably angry and laser clear about how my white privilege and racism had impacted not only her but the larger local and national teams, as well as conference participants.
>
> When she voiced her thoughts loudly and in front of the group, I chose to respond by shutting her out.
>
> She approached me after the meeting and I told her I didn't think what she was saying was all on me, and I refused to accept responsibility for it. The more animated she became, the colder and more distant I responded. This served my purpose of reclaiming power and agency by appearing cool and rational. And, in effect, I pathologized her behaviors as overly emotional and mentally unstable.
>
> Looking back on my life, becoming distant and unemotional was a strategy I used in arguments with my family. I'm-not-talking-to-you icy silence was my way of getting

back at people who hurt me. As a white woman, the power to control my emotions and socially isolate others was a helpful tool I developed, especially when those hurting me were physically larger men and adults. I also used this with my sister. If we were arguing and she was screaming, I knew the way to infuriate her was to calmly respond or even smile condescendingly. My parents would see this and likely think she was the one causing the problems.

White cultural norms dictate that the most reasoned, unemotional response is most valid. This manipulative tactic can help preserve our sense of "niceness" while quietly or silently lashing out. One of the reasons that images of a white teen boy in the MAGA hat smirking at Nathan Phillips while he drums at the National Mall caused such a reaction is because that condescending smile is something People of Color have seen so many times before.[12] As white children, we are taught to wield that tool in asserting our power over people. It is an expression of contempt that signals white children to utilize their power over People of Color in palpable ways.

Ilsa continued, explaining how she triangulated to reaffirm her identity as an anti-racist ally.

After this conversation with the Woman of Color, I spoke with other white women who were there, looking to affirm I wasn't *that* bad. They assured me that, although I had made some mistakes, the Woman of Color needed to deal with her personal issues that had nothing to do with me. I talked with my partner and my father, both white men, who also assured me this had less to do with racism than with her personal issues (despite the fact they didn't know her and only knew my side of the story). I called and met with several People of Color, both men and women, who were at the meeting. Each had a different take, but on the whole, this was how I reassured myself I was not a bad person. I never circled back to the Woman of Color.

The fact that Ilsa centered her own identity as a good person and good anti-racist in her reflection on the experience demonstrates one of the behaviors of white women in the phase we call Defense. Instead, she could have simply listened to the concerns raised and responded thoughtfully, rather than associating the accusations with a personal label of racist she felt the need to defend.

Final Thoughts

I immediately and quickly answered a Person of Color's question I saw as challenging my authority.

I'm speaking loudly and more than others to make sure the "most important points" in this meeting get made.

I reacted automatically by clutching my purse when a Latino man walked toward me.

I bumped into an Indigenous person as I walked quickly through the mall because they failed to yield the right of way to me.

All of these are behaviors common in Defense. As white women take on the world, we don't notice or care much who stands in our way. This way of being feels powerful compared to earlier stages and we hold on tight! Transitioning to the next phase is hard because in many ways it feels like relinquishing some of our hard-fought accomplishments.

Feeling Defense

If you can, stand with your knees bent and feet slightly apart, one in front of the other. Lift your arms up in fists like a boxer in the ring. Hunch your shoulders and get ready to fight. Move around punching an occasional jab, imagining these directed toward men. Connect with other white women with a fist bump or locking arms for a moment. Make eye contact and smile at them. Imagine encountering a Person of Color, smiling to their face, then bouncing backward, to the side, or even behind their back with a couple of punches directed toward them.

- As you moved in this gesture, what felt natural to you? What felt unnatural?

- What feelings came up for you? Where did these feelings land in your body?
- If you were with other women when you tried this gesture, how did their bodies feel and look to you? How did you feel toward them?

Some have pointed out that a true defensive gesture involves blocking rather than punching. The intersection of domination and subordination we're attempting to embody involves both.

Strategic Questions for Defense

- How have you been hurt by sexism? How have you hurt others because of your own internalized sexism?
- Tell me about how you have navigated sexism in your personal/professional life.
- Share how you feel when you are told you are racist.
- What stories are in your head when you are told you are a racist?
- When it comes to struggles you've faced, what do you want people to know about you that they may not?
- How do you want to be seen by people? By People of Color in particular? Why?
- What kinds of relationships do you want with People of Color?
- What values and strengths will help you form these relationships?

7

Projection

*It won't help much to be prepared to face Jane Elliott.
This elderly woman will tear down any shield. Even we,
the spectators in BLUE EYED, can't get rid of this feeling of
uneasiness, embarrassment, anxiety and utterly helpless hatred
when she starts keeping people down, humiliating them,
deriding them, incapacitating them. No doubt about this:
for three quarters of the time in this documentary Jane Elliott
is the meanest, the lowest, the most detestful, the most
hypocritical human being hell has ever spit back on earth.
But she should be an example for all of us.*

— *Stuttgarter Zeitung*

A s the name of this phase suggests, white women in the Projection stage of development have an outward focus. Instead of showing up in new and creative ways that vary with context, in Projection, we're trying to memorize the "rules" of anti-racism. The idea of a set of rules comes from readings and checklists that detail what People of Color want from white people and identify the ways we may unintentionally uphold racism. For example, we may read about tone policing for the first time and broadly apply this idea to mean people should speak however they want to fight racism, with or without regard for our shared humanity. We understand new concepts at a surface level and can use the language of anti-racism without processing any deeper.

107

The characteristic assumptions and behaviors of white women in this stage stem primarily from how we want to appear, the identity we want to project to the world, as we progress in our understanding of whiteness. We love the fact that we get recognized for showing up to do anti-racism work, even though People of Color rarely receive the same kind of accolades (and white women know better than to say out loud that we want the gold star for our allyship). We are quick to point out the failings of other white people and frequently feel deep shame or even self-hatred about our own mistakes. We may look to People of Color to affirm for us how we project our identity as allies and work harder to be seen as racial justice advocates than we work in advocating for racial justice.

In Projection, white women have heightened awareness of racism and white privilege, while now downplaying the role of internalized sexism in our lives. For the first time, we have a multicultural understanding of racial experiences, rather than the monocultural worldview found in the first three phases. In other words, we grasp the concept that people in the United States may have very different experiences because of race. We recognize that institutional racism matters, rather than simply seeing all experiences as related to the individual.

To move into the stage we call Projection, a white woman typically must have a significant event or person in our life that causes our eyes to open to the reality of racism in a way we had never before considered. Unlike our personal understanding of sexism, we must believe the reality of experiences of oppression outside of our own, even as our white experiences are reinforced as part of "normal" life.

Dena explained the difference between understanding sexism and white privilege:

> I think there's a difference between the internal strength that I had gained from a Women's Studies perspective from my college days. I literally grew from inside. As opposed to my whiteness [which] I know is sort of more external

as [people and systems] relate to me.... So, [there is] this internal strength [from understanding sexism], and this external white power that I get that I have to be conscious of. What I'm trying to say is the internal strength of the voice or whatever it is, is on a cellular level. My whiteness is not on a cellular level; it's like a cloak that I wear but I have to remember it is on. I have to keep remembering, keep remembering, keep remembering.

While recognizing sexism can give us a sense of internal strength, acknowledging the way that society affords us benefits because we are white feels like something we're given, not something we control. What Dena refers to as a cloak we have to continually remember we are wearing has a deep and profound influence on the way we move through the world. However hard it may be for us to see our privilege, it is usually obvious to People of Color. More often than not, the people opening our eyes to the world of racism are people we have been taught to disbelieve or have stereotyped as less intelligent. Projection comes only after we have woken to our white privilege and keep remembering it is there.

For white women, sexism can be an entry point into better understanding white privilege. Robin shared an example of this:

If someone's trying to give me some feedback and I'm not getting it, then I just have to imagine a man is saying to me right now what I'm saying to this person, and (snaps fingers) just like that I've got it...Like when white people say I don't feel safe talking about racism, and I think, imagine trying to talk to a man about sexism and he's saying he doesn't feel safe talking about sexism with me. For one second, I wouldn't entertain that as legitimate. So that's helped me.

In Projection, white women may feel guilt or anger at our previous ignorance and our actions that unconsciously perpetuated racism. In a self-reinforcing cycle, the more open we are to learn about racism, the more People of Color will open up to us about their experiences, the more we might wonder, "How could I have possibly missed this?" Many women in our focus groups talked about how difficult it was to not judge ourselves or become defensive as we move into Projection because we're now conscious of our mistakes in earlier stages. Our internalized sexism can contribute to seeing ourselves as horrible people.

Ilana stated, "The times in my life I have the most white shame have been in multiracial feminist settings where I just now learned that I'm a racist, and I just now learned that reverse racism doesn't exist."

We may direct our shame internally or lash out at others or both. Many white women can relate to a time when we lectured our family members on how horribly racist they are. Or we withdrew from people we loved because we couldn't stand the white privilege we now recognized in them. Laura shared, "There were times when I would come home and cry and get in arguments with the family to the point where I'd have to leave and go check in a hotel."

No matter how well we understand that racism is an institutional problem, we may still feel guilt around our personal collusion. Shifting into a place of anger and wanting to do something, anything, and do it NOW, helps alleviate some of the negative feelings about oneself. This is also a characteristic of Projection. We're going to go out there and change the world. We just need someone to tell us how.

Following the "Rules" of Anti-Racist Allyship

Many People of Color have clearly articulated what they want from white allies, including skills such as listening to and believing People of Color's experiences, examining impact rather than intention, advocating for equity in organizations (especially in spaces where no PoC are present), and calling out racism in all-white groups. Understanding and acting on these guidelines are important. Like learning to write, we have to first learn the rules to recognize when we can break them or use them more flexibly. True anti-racism work involves compassion, empathy, and authenticity, and is more creative and responsive than any checklist. But the phase of Projection is all about learning the list.

White people's fatigue can also account for why we very quickly want to figure out what to do and rules for doing it right. In the book *Occupying Privilege: Conversations on Love, Race and Liberation*, Danny Hoch makes this point as he and JLove Calderón are discussing gentrification:

> Well, it's interesting what your questions are, even just there…"Does that mean I should move back home?" or "What does that mean?" There's a writer named Adrianne Piper and she talks about something called white people's fatigue, which means that we just want an answer, a quick fix answer that absolves us of our participation in racism. In other words, "So what does that mean? Should I NOT vote for Obama? What should I do? Just TELL me what to do! I don't actually want to do the work; I just want to know what to do. Tell me what to do so I'm not guilty." Because white folks are tired at having the finger pointed at us. Where do we go from here? We displace more people. We continue to affirm our entitlement as white progressives. We feel great, and we pat ourselves on the back because we elected a Black president, and, therefore, we're all revolutionaries. We continue to do our good work on the left. And we continue to destroy other people's lives while helping some.[1]

Instead of sitting with the discomfort that our new knowledge of racism brings up in our minds, instead of staying with that twisted feeling in our guts, white women in the stage of Projection very quickly want to turn to action that lets us off the hook. In this phase, we tend to think we can "fix" racism. In contrast, People of Color have been surviving and living with the daily indignities and resulting discomfort of racism for generations.

As discussed in the Defense chapter, because white women have had to work harder than white men to be seen, heard, and taken seriously, we often develop perfectionist habits. Whiteness reinforces this, as we are rewarded for perfectly crafted final products and are held up as examples of what it means to be an "ideal" woman. In the stage of Projection, we have just begun to understand white privilege. Yet we try to now act in "perfectly" anti-racist ways, wanting to project the "perfect" image of an ally. This might result in caution around sharing our actual thoughts in cross-race dialogues. We may pause, trying to say things in just the right way. Rigid and dogmatic perfectionism prevents us from making true internal change and keeps us focused instead on external rewards, such as accolades from People of Color.

Terrie spoke about community organizing she was doing with People of Color around homelessness. "I'm working hard as an anti-racist and I'm even getting validation that I'm doing great work. It's not even at my job, you know. It's in the community." At the same time, she didn't show up authentically or bring part of her skill set to the group. "Typically, I'm not the person who volunteers to take the minutes. I'm not the first person in any workplace who says, 'Oh, I'll maintain those lists.' Suddenly I was doing all this stuff very voluntarily and in a pleasing way and was very pleased to do it. But like I said, I don't feel I used any of the real skills I had to be able to benefit this body of folks."

Terrie was quick to do whatever she was asked, and no more, failing to bring her full skill set to the group and finding herself doing work typically relegated to women. Many white women in the stage we call Projection keep quiet around People of Color as we carefully try to follow their leadership and not make any mistakes. We may try to make all People of Color happy. We try to guess what they want to hear or agree to do things for them we're not particularly skilled at, and then struggle to develop authentic relationships as a result. This is again rooted in proving we're not racist, and, therefore, a good person. We assume any feedback we get from People of Color is completely true, even when we get contradictory messages from different people. When this happens, it may confuse us because we still see People of Color as monolithic rather than individuals with shared racialized identities.

Depending on a Person of Color's stage of development, they may want us to avoid bringing up race, love when we shame other white people, expect us to follow the rules of allyship, get mad at us for not being authentic, want us to invite other white people gently into social justice work, or have none of these expectations of white women. We may try to be the best anti-racist ally of all time by doing whatever People of Color want, regardless of our critical thinking. As Katy pointed out, "Compared to the other stages, I think Projection is a relational dynamic term. You have to have something to project on, to do a projection."

She spoke about a complex situation at work when a Woman of Color shared an experience of racism and then expected Katy to do something about it as a white ally and her supervisor.

What I didn't understand was that she had an expectation beyond me saying, "Yeah, that really does sound like she is perceiving you based on race and not just based on the work you are doing, and that's really awful. And you are doing a great job working with this family and navigating this situation. And we support 100% your assessment of what's happening here." To me, that was that. I didn't know there was an expectation of a next step until later. So, I felt very like, wait a minute, I knew that there was racism. That wasn't enough to know there was racism? That sense of, "What do you expect from me? I'm still a white person. I can't take the next step, but I could at least figure it out that it was there."

I wanted some sort of credit for going there. For bringing it up even though I clearly didn't know what to do with it once we were there. You tell me what it looks like for me to be an ally. Tell me. Tell me the rules. I thought I was doing it. So, there is that desire for a very clear workflow of "if…then," white anti-racist social worker. I did want a very clear rubric of what to do that was right, and I wanted her to tell me what it was, and when she wasn't telling me what it was, I was very frustrated. You just tell me what to

do. Would you just tell me what to do? I don't know which
way is the right way.

As evidenced in Katy's story, not only do we want a clear set of
rules, but we also may feel entitled to support from People of
Color in figuring this out. The rules of anti-racist allyship are so
important to us in Projection we may think that if we mess up, we
can't be an ally.

Dualistic Thinking

Part of the problem with following the rules so closely is that Projection mirrors the white dominant culture of right/wrong and
either/or. In conversations about racism, white women may be
told we can't talk about sexism because we are just trying to use
our target identities to get out of talking about our privilege. We
frequently believe we have to choose either racism or sexism, and
at this point in our development, we think racism is the bigger
problem. Any pain we feel around sexism gets tucked away and
later leaks out in all sorts of toxic ways.

Another bind of dualistic thinking comes up with our emotions. Many People of Color have shared the negative impact
white women's tears have on group dynamics where our needs
are prioritized. More is written about this in the chapter, White
Women's Tears. When we internalize the idea that we shouldn't
cry as a hard and fast rule, we believe crying would mean we were
trying to manipulate the conversation by having people pay attention to our emotions. Instead, we stuff down our emotions and
end up engaging from an intellectual place, rather than with our
hearts. Then we find out that being too intellectual and not willing to connect with the pain of racism is also harmful to authentic
relationships.

With more interest in supporting the Black Lives Matter movement, white people have got the message it is time to sit down,
listen, and follow the leadership of Black, Indigenous, and People
of Color. At the same time, we're being told our silence implies
consent and we need to speak up. Our internalized superiority

may still be telling us we deserve to be able to voice our opinions or that if we don't speak up, the most important points won't be made (because who else is going to be this brilliant?). Without utilizing our creative thinking to figure out whether or not to speak up in a given moment based on the context, white women in Projection can easily use these competing messages to excuse our inaction altogether.

There are many other examples where the either/or bind leaves us confused, inauthentic, or frustrated with ourselves. White women may move back into the stage of Defense as we feel *damned if I do, damned if I don't.*

Competing to be the Best White Person

Because white women in the Projection phase are focused on how we appear to others, the external validation we receive from People of Color is very important. We may find ourselves competing for recognition. This is encouraged by sexism in the workplace, where we've had to compete to get ahead.

Having now learned about our whiteness and institutional racism, we realize we should not exert our superiority over People of Color. However, internalized superiority we've spent a lifetime learning, superiority housed deep in our bodies, is not something we can shrug off easily. Instead, it now shows up in our interactions with other white people.

Christine shared an example of how she exerted this in her relationships with white men in workshops on race,

> There are times when I want the angry white man because then I would just go after him. Like I would just go, "Come on angry white man, because I'm ready for you." I won't lie: that righteous indignation felt good. I would point out how terrible that angry white man was. And then I realized that, too, was part of my internalized oppression. That was me fighting against it. There are so many white men that I wished I could go and apologize to. It wasn't about me trying to undo racism. It wasn't really about helping them

become my partner in fighting racism. It was about me ex-
orcising my internalized oppression demon.

In the competition for the anti-racist gold star, we may insist other
white people not speak for us. We see ourselves as individuals,
outside of the white group norm (i.e., racist), even though we can
name privileges afforded to us because of our white group mem-
bership.

Ilsa's story illustrates this.

I was in a workshop exploring the dynamics of racism and
chose to tell the group that I was feeling competitive with
other white people in the room and had observed my desire to distance myself from a few of them because of the
mistakes I perceived they'd made. I said something along
the lines of, "I'm noticing I'm doing this thing we white
people often do..."

Later, two of the white women in the group asked that I
speak for my experiences, not theirs. As they barely spoke
with me beyond that, I assumed they, too, were trying to
distance themselves from me. This was, ironically, the very
thing I was noticing in myself. I got the distinct impression
they'd rather not be associated with a white person like
me who was *clearly* less adept at this work than they were.
Even as I share this, I'm pissed that they thought they were
better than me, which indicates I'm the one who is actually
better than them!

In this example, the two white women who confronted Ilsa were
concerned that other people in the group would see them all the
same. And Ilsa gets upset, assuming they think they're better than
her, a characteristic response of Projection. This then becomes a
cycle where we try to prove we're the best anti-racist in the room
and end up creating more divisions between white people rather
than working together against racism. (If we could all just agree
Tilman and Ilsa are obviously the best white anti-racists in the
world it would solve a lot of these problems.)

The idea of "dueling Projection" came up in our focus groups. As one person asserts their superiority, someone else responds in kind. We're often passive-aggressive in our approach, offering "feedback" or asking a question without genuine curiosity. The group was able to easily identify times when we'd tried to prove our anti-racist approach is best. Chris shared this story:

> There is a protest every year in Emeryville at the Bayshore Mall, San Francisco, because they built the shopping mall on an Ohlone burial mound that is thousands of years old and they just knocked it down. The burial ground is still there and there are still many ancestral remains there in addition to other extremely important parts of the Ohlone culture. So, the Ohlone people organize this protest every year and they have a big ceremony on Shellmound Way and let people know that the mall is built on the burial grounds.
>
> I was there and had been there for the last couple of years. I tend to wait for people in their cars, like when they are stopped at the red light, and I say, "Do you know that this mall is built on a cemetery?" They can't usually hear what I'm saying so they roll down their window and then I say this mall is built on a burial ground of the Ohlone people and I give them a flyer really fast. I devised this method after trying first to say Ohlone burial ground, and I noticed that people respond most positive to cemetery because it registers very quickly. And then once I get their attention, I can explain it's a burial ground.
>
> A young white woman came up to me and we had a Projection-off. She said, "Excuse me, can I ask you a question?" and I said, "Oh yes, of course."
>
> She said, "Why are you saying cemetery?"
>
> And I said, "Oh well, I've been doing this for a couple of years and I've just found that it's the most effective word and it really catches people's attention and then I can explain to them about the Ohlone..."

"You know I really feel that you are not being true to the Ohlone people and how they would describe this. You know this is a burial mound not a cemetery. I just don't really agree with your method."

I was really pissed off at this point. We exchanged a lot of words and then I said, "Why don't you show me your method and I will do that?"

She said, "No, I have to go over there…I can't. I just think the way you are talking about it is not accurate."

And I said, "*Accurate*. That's a very white word." And that was the end of our conversation.

This kind of competitive exchange hurts the movement to end racism and can be quite exhausting to People of Color. White people in the Projection stage often take up space by naming the multiple ways we are recognizing our white privilege or pointing out all of the *other* white people who are the problem in the workplace. This virtue signaling is intended to show everyone how much we understand and how amazing we are as allies, and it is a sign of our internalized sense of superiority as well as insecurity from internalized sexism. We can alienate other white people from movements for justice through our righteousness and create environments of "us vs. them."

Ours are the loudest voices interrupting meetings or posting comments in the chat, truly believing this is what it means to be an anti-racist accomplice. People of Color, who often can't afford to alienate white coworkers, end up silenced or having to smooth things over. When we shame other white people in the workplace, they typically go to their Colleagues of Color for reassurance, creating even more burden for those already facing racism.

Relating to Black Men

The context of racism and sexism makes white women's relationships with Men of Color, particularly Black men, challenging. If a white woman comes to the awareness of her whiteness before understanding sexism, she is unlikely to even notice this happening.

Feminist movements have frequently failed to take into account the lynching of Black men because of false rape accusations by white women. Anti-racism movements have failed to fully address sexism directed at white women and Women of Color. Before Projection, we may be unaware of these dynamics or downplay them. Now there is a new hyper-focus that can result in our feeling frozen. Even as we write this, we notice our nervousness in wanting to name an important intersection of oppressions but knowing it would be easier and more comfortable for us as white women to ignore. We rarely navigate this tension well in the moment.

Mallory stated,

> It feels like that particular kind of racism against African Americans...particularly men, is so violent and dangerous and scary that I have to make allowances, and I have to not add to it. My boss right now is an African American man, and I can ask him for things, and I can say I don't particularly think that was a good idea, but if I get any kind of frown or anything, I back off. But other men in my life I'm happy to just continue to pursue it until I get my way, or I get heard at least.

At times, Mallory's approach is a genuinely effective way to navigate racism and not use her privilege to bulldoze through with an idea. It might also mean she silences a good idea she would otherwise bring to the table for fear of appearing racist. It is important for white women to be aware of when we are trying to offer a critique that is useful to the conversation and when we are trying to exert control over a Black person and re-center whiteness.

Many of the women in our focus groups recognized times when they did not speak up about sexism because of the race of a man. Beth Yohe named this as an area of struggle for her, and she looks to Women of Color to validate her understanding:

> The last several years I've had experiences with Men of Color in spaces where I really experience the maleness and feel like I can't say anything because of the race dynamic.

Some of it I recognize as me really trying to figure out like what of this is race, and what is my whiteness in terms of expectations of behaviors or how I'm proceeding, and what of this really truly is about sexism. [I've got] the messages *"Well, you know that person really has issues with white women."* I can't bring up something because maybe it really is about my whiteness. So, I'm feeling really conflicted and feeling like I'm getting those messages from other white women that, okay, it must be me...

I was interning at the Social Justice Training Institute (SJTI) and I experienced one of the participants in that way. An African American male that clearly was in a lot of pain, and SJTI is about race, right? And he really showed up in the amount of space that he was taking...I really felt like there was a significant amount of maleness happening there and I felt like I couldn't say anything. I was so relieved when two other Women of Color named it...I felt like I could never have said it, and I had to be validated...

And I had that come up subsequently in a couple of other spaces. And that's really where I'm struggling now. Trying to figure out how I parse that out and how I can get to a place where I can speak my experience of sexism clearly, while still holding race.

We've seen this happen in many social justice workshops. Black men or other Men of Color will talk about their experiences and perspectives, while white women listen quietly. On the one hand, this serves to counter racism, centering the voices of those most impacted. On the other, white women are then given a pass in having to take risks articulating our thinking. We fail to develop relationships founded in mutuality when we don't talk about our own racial stories and thereby perpetuate the idea that we don't have a story to tell because we are the racial "norm." In addition, the man's voice is again seen as the most valuable, continuing a pattern of patriarchy.

In anti-racism work, both white men and Men of Color often

get more recognition. Peggy pointed out her collusion with this due to sexism. "And I find that when I'm looking at who I think does the anti-racist work really well, I tend to start with men. So internalized sexism...I feel quite angry about a lot of the men who have done anti-racist work if they've ripped off my work, which has happened. But still, I tend to think of them as sort of the most effective."

Chris talked about another challenge with the race and gender dynamics in activist circles. "This person had sexually harassed a woman. She showed us the text messages that he had sent, and it was clearly inappropriate. But none of us were in any position to be able to call him out because he's a Black man and she's a white woman and isn't that just the classic thing? And so, we just shared stories and that was the end of that."

Katy spoke about how, within a heterosexual framework, it was easier for her to relate to Black male coworkers than to Women of Color. "To me, working with an African American male is much easier because there is a gender divide. It feels like there is a place of contact because he and I are both heterosexual. We didn't have an affair, that's not what I'm saying. There is this concept of being drawn toward even though there's a racial divide. I can bring myself to [a Person of Color] if we relate sexually, or I can bring myself as a helper or a healer."

Patriarchy defines our role as women as the lover, helper, or healer—in other words, providing a service to men. Because this resonates with how we navigate sexism, it may feel more familiar and comfortable. White women in Projection also worry about being called a racist if we show up in anything but a subservient role with Men of Color because we are depending on them to affirm our goodness. White women's lack of self-reflection as we deny or downplay our privilege in these relationships can easily result in danger to the Black men involved. Throughout history, we have quickly shifted from fun, flirtatious relationships to threatening Black men's lives when they fail to acquiesce to our demands (even when we make these demands as "requests" with a smile and a wink).

It is imperative to listen to and believe Black men to end racism. However, white women do a disservice to movements for justice when we passively listen to and follow the lead of Black men no matter what, because that is a good allyship rule we learned, and our internalized sexism dictates this role. To move toward the next stages, we also need to be authentically engaged in dialogue and critical thinking; to take risks to share our own stories appropriately and not avoid naming sexist harassment we wouldn't accept from white men. We must engage in potentially difficult interactions with Black men to unpack the intersecting dynamics of racism and sexism to better collaborate in the fight for justice.

The Helper

In Projection, white women can get into relationships with People of Color that are unhealthy for everyone involved. Due to our desire to be good allies, combined with our internalized sexism, we often choose to be in a helper role. Because of our internalized superiority, we situate ourselves as doing something for or on behalf of People of Color, rather than with or alongside them.

Chris told us about a friendship she had with a Woman of Color where institutional racism and internalized sexism came into play.

> I became friends with someone based on talking about her experience of racism. That was really a terrible, horrible way to try to start a friendship. In the beginning, I felt like I was the best ally. The best white person ally. She would literally tell me, "You are the one."...She never would come to me. I would always go to where she was on her schedule, on her time. She had complete control of me and my time in terms of our relationship. I was totally available.
>
> There's this dynamic that happens between People of Color and white people with anti-racist organizing that's really unhealthy for everybody. Because of the internalized sexism, I think, "That just must have been me being racist."

That makes you unable to have that conversation about "What was that other creepy thing I was picking up on?" There's been so many times in my life when this kind of fly trap thing is really visceral for me, and I don't think it's created by People of Color. In anti-racism work, this set of relationships exist and people get sucked into it. It's like roles we come to play, and I feel like I've been sucked into it so many times.

In my case, what it really took was a Person of Color, a Woman of Color who really cared about me saying, "Listen to me. This is insane. You have to stop. See what is happening here. This Person of Color is taking advantage of you." It had to be a PoC who said that to get me out. If a white person had said that this PoC is taking advantage of you, which was an accurate description of what was happening, I would have been like, "No, no, no. That's racist and you're being racist and I'm being racist if I listen to you." It was my partner [a Woman of Color], again and again, shaking me out of these situations saying, "Chris, what are you doing?"

Tilman shared a time when this was a pattern for her as well,

About 20 years ago, I became involved in an organizing effort to ban the embargo against Cuba. This was a strong and visionary collective of women, led by Women of Color, that took trips to Cuba to build solidarity, bring needed materials to Cuban women and children, and to learn firsthand what life was like to educate people in the United States.

I was very much embedded in the Projection phase of my development, and I learned and practiced the allyship rules as I had memorized them. The key rule for me was to follow the direction of Women of Color no matter what they asked me to do, or what they were doing themselves. The second rule was to ferret out any other white women (and Women of Color) who might not be exhibiting an "appropriate" degree of anti-racism practice as dictated by the women in leadership.

The way that this manifested was to either freeze out certain women who did not fit into the core group, to chastise women who were displaying their white privilege, and critique those who appeared to be capitulating to white supremacist ways of being. I would be given a directive to talk to someone, and I would do it. I didn't question, I didn't even ask why. To show my commitment, I understood that I was to "correct" the other white woman at all costs, even if it meant humiliation, and that is what I did. It took many years for me to understand the damage that these confrontations caused, to others, to me, and to the group. Instead of bringing us together and making us stronger, it served to position me in the "best anti-racist" position at the cost of the integrity of our purpose and work.

Both Chris and Tilman's stories demonstrate patterns we see in the first three stages in relation to white men, but in the Projection stage, the authority is now relegated to People of Color. We elevate, don't question, and agree to all requests. Chris and Tilman willingly engaged in these relationships because of the accolades they received. All of the hard work we're doing to end racism and the People of Color in our lives we can point to as proof of our anti-racist identity amplify the sense of "goodness" we white women continually strive for. Importantly, we must recognize, as Chris points out, these dynamics were not created by the People of Color or white women involved. They are patterns of relationship white women developed over time in reaction to patriarchy and that reinforce our sense of superiority over other white people.

Final Thoughts

Like learning any new behavior, we must practice before it becomes automatic. When learning to drive a car, for example, we might first feel overwhelmed by all of the rules of the road and the potential to cause life-threatening accidents. We carefully navigate all of the controls, hopefully with a good instructor or two. We might be extra aware of and frustrated with people not following the rules, like cyclists who make a rolling stop at a stop sign. We rely on external validation, someone giving us a license or complimenting our driving.

Eventually, we become so comfortable that we can't remember how we got home some days. We can drive a car completely different from our own and even fairly easily learn new rules in other cities or countries. We don't need to be told we are good drivers.

This progress from conscious, intentional action to instinctive is similar to moving from Projection to Balance. The learning that happens in Projection is a necessary part of our growth. Unfortunately, many white women who are concerned with racial justice stay in this phase because of the accolades we receive. We look to external rewards rather than internal strength because we see how white men have gained power in this way. We may not be able to imagine another way of being in "the work."

Feeling Projection

Sit up straight or stand if you are able. Tilt your head slightly so you are looking down on others. Stretch out one arm and point down at people. Put a judgmental scowl on your face. Now move around and imagine silently point out all of the ways other white people are racist. Picture encountering a Person of Color and going in whatever direction they indicate. Occasionally point back at yourself with disdain and feel the weight of ending racism resting solely on your shoulders.

- As you held this gesture, what felt natural to you? What felt unnatural?
- What feelings came up for you? Where did these feelings land in your body?
- If you were with other women when you tried this gesture, how did their bodies feel and look to you? How did you feel toward them?

Strategic Questions for Projection

- What behaviors are you doing that might be pushing other white people away from racial justice, rather than bringing them in? What rewards or recognition do you get for continuing these behaviors (especially from People of Color)?
- Where do you feel confused or frustrated by rules or advice that is seemingly contradictory in anti-racism work?
- When have you felt a pang in your gut or some other dissonance in your body around following the "rules of anti-racism" in a way that doesn't feel authentic?
- What motivates you to practice and work on racial justice? How do you create support and resilience for yourself to stay motivated?
- Talk about your past and present relationships with People of Color. What are the characteristics of your true friendships? If you do not have these characteristics in your relationships with People of Color, what keeps you from changing this? What are you most afraid of discovering?
- When and why do feelings of superiority to People of Color come up for you? What do you do with these feelings?
- Do you ever feel you are superior to other white people? When and why?
- How do you see sexism showing up in your efforts to address racism?
- How have you hurt others with your white privilege? How have you been hurt by white privilege?

8

Balance

How can we make it possible for everyone to live
as whole person, to have self-determination,
to be treated with dignity and respect, and to have access
to material necessities as well as joy?

— Suzanne Pharr

THE PHASE WE CALL Balance is the first point where white women can consistently hold space for, or balance, both the reality of sexism and racism. Balance also implies a state of teetering on the edge of the canyon, rather than standing on solid ground. We have to work to engage our core to keep from falling back to an earlier phase, making a conscious effort to analyze and respond thoughtfully in any given situation.

Balance is a state where white women are actively aware of power dynamics in the systems we operate within and are practicing skills so we show up in ways more closely aligned with our values of equity and justice. At this point, white women have an understanding of interpersonal, cultural, institutional, and structural racism. We can point out ways we have personally internalized white superiority and see the connection between the systems that have privileged us and our resulting behaviors and beliefs. We can also grasp how we have internalized sexism and the ways this is reinforced by the systemic oppression of women. We more easily recognize how both internalized superiority and internalized oppression harm us and how experiencing both systemic racism and sexism amplifies harm for Women of Color.

Most white women wake up every morning in Immersion. But, having been taught racist and sexist ideas our entire lives, white women in Balance know the likelihood of our gut reaction or intuition being shaped by those frames. When told to "trust our gut," we rightfully wonder, "What if my gut is racist?"

Up to this point in our development, most of the focus has been external: white women looking for affirmation from white men, from each other, from society, and from People of Color to attest to the fact that we are good people or are doing anti-racism work in the "right way." Peggy illustrates the new mindset of Balance when she questions the use of the word "accountability" in social justice circles.

> But holding anybody accountable...I don't do it, and I can't do it. I just don't know what it means...People get this word and then it has a self-righteousness about it. Accountable to whom for what? Nobody ever answers it in a way that makes sense to me.
>
> So, let's say you're running a school and you have to [follow] all these policies. You've got all these constituencies. You have to decide which ones you will prioritize when you make your policy decisions. That's what's being accountable. It's balancing power relations...Just trying to balance out the power relations so that you're working for the decent survival of everybody.
>
> I don't make any sense out of that word, but it triggers me; it makes me angry. I think it's been over-used by people who don't know what the hell they're talking about. They just got hold of this word and it has to do with setting other people right. It doesn't have to do with deep knowing of the kind you're working for here. Self-awareness. Awareness of bigger systems, placing one's self within them, and ending up being as effective as you can as a human being for yourself and for others.

Counter-intuitively, as the external focus shifts to the internal, we see that we ourselves are not at the heart of the matter. In other words, the choices we make are not based on what others will think about us, whether we have the right accountability, how we will look, or whether we will receive any kind of affirmation for our efforts. We understand that our liberation is tied to others, and we center the voices and needs of those most marginalized in our daily efforts to end oppression. Much of what we do for racial equity is in relationship with People of Color and, therefore, necessarily changes between people, cultural groups, and various causes. As Peggy so wisely offered in our focus group, "I used to want to be important; now I just want to be useful."

Driving in the Ocean

Getting to Balance on a regular basis involves practicing new skills, like learning to drive, but ones we need to relearn every day as if there were no road. Indeed, the society we live in constantly reinforces staying in Immersion. Perhaps a more apt metaphor would be trying to learn to drive a car through an ocean with the current flowing against us.

As we practice, we can hopefully get to Balance more readily, but we need to know the components that help us get there. More importantly, we actually need to feel that the incentive of living in a more just society outweighs the roadblocks of oppression and rewards we get for colluding with systems that privilege us.

Mab Segrest captures the idea of living into a new way of being in her book, *Memoir of a Race Traitor*, where she shared her response to the oral portion of her green belt test in karate,

> "What do you want to learn from the art of karate?"
>
> "How not to quit at something that comes very hard to me…How to have the mind in the body, that can send and receive messages from fingers and knees and neck and toes. How to build from basics, not jump over them."[1]

Balance does not occur by happenstance. In this phase, white women are diligent about strengthening habits and internalizing skills that will provide us with the needed awareness and resilience to remain in Balance more often and return to it with more ease.

Paulo Freire's model of Praxis—theory, practice, and reflection—can help us stay in Balance. We move through this cycle continuously and choose to do so intentionally with discipline and focus, toward transformation. When any one of these three components goes missing, we tend to retreat to a former phase.[2]

This phase differs from Projection in that it goes beyond a formulaic understanding of allyship. White women in this stage make purposeful decisions that align our actions with our values. Living in a way that is not oppressive is much less about anti-oppression "work" and much more about who and how we are in the world. As white women in this stage strategically weigh decisions, we are focused on the impact, rather than how we will be regarded.

Mallory spoke of the disequilibrium and intentionality involved in Balance.

> I'm realizing that [within a] relationship that I have with a student of mine and his family, most of the time I'm interacting with them I'm probably in Balance. Sometimes I feel like I'm on a knife edge, like I'm going to screw this up any second. And it's kind of this swaying motion...
>
> The family is African [from Somalia]. There are nine kids in the family and the third oldest child is a student of mine and has been for four years, and...he calls me grandmother. He has adopted me as his grandmother and wouldn't let me not be his grandmother until I finally gave up and agreed to be his grandmother. And I also teach two of his siblings, and now I'm teaching his mom how to read and write and speak English.
>
> And so, there's that sort of knife edge feeling...this is a minefield. I live in one culture and they live in another, and they don't have any money...and I can retire now if I want. In lots of different ways, I'm Christian, they're Muslim. My hair is everywhere, their hair is bound. I sit cross legged on the floor and they sit on the floor, but the women

would never sit cross legged. There's just like these massive differences.

And there's also a lot of love and consideration and concern and worry that we all have for each other…And it feels like this…is a place where I know I could screw up on a daily basis. And yeah, there's a little tiny piece of me that says, "Okay run, stay out of that! Don't go where you're going to look like a stupid fool and hurt people that you care about. You need to leave!" But most of me is just doing it. Just going ahead and doing it.

I get so much out of my relationship with that family. It's enormously rewarding for me to have children in my life again…and to watch them grow up. It's really clearly not charity unless it's they who are giving charity to me. But at the same time, I can be really useful. They have passports and I can read the English and explain how to fill out the forms. So, I understand the things that we do for each other.

And when it feels not like a knife edge, when it feels like I'm not on the verge of hurting somebody, it's when…I can keep in mind my privilege, and I can keep in mind their struggle, and I can keep in mind my pain for losing my father and my daughter in the same year, basically, and getting a little bit of a family back.

Racism amplifies the complexity of the relationships we have with People of Color. We're constantly navigating across our differences, and in Balance, we willingly sit in the discomfort, or on the knife's edge, rather than expecting People of Color to become more similar to us or beholden to us. We value our differences and seek to better understand how people navigate oppressive realities. We recognize that at any moment, our lack of understanding and internalized superiority could lead to a fissure in the relationship that we will be responsible (and may be unable) to mend.

Figure 8.1. Hayes' ADDRESSING Model

A	Age
D	Developmental Disability
D	Disability (Acquired)
R	Religion
E	Ethnicity & Race
S	Sexual Orientation
S	Socioeconomic Status
I	Indigenous Heritage
N	National Origin & Language
G	Gender

Intersectionality

White women in Balance seek to understand the ways multiple dimensions of identity influence one's access to privilege and power. Pamela Hays' ADDRESSING model names these multiple determinants where laws and practices provide privilege or disadvantage. A framework that claims *either* racism *or* sexism is more important, has an end result of rendering Women of Color invisible.[3]

Kimberlé Crenshaw first coined the term *intersectionality* to describe how anti-discrimination policies designed to benefit women in companies included only white women. At the same time, racial equity policies primarily benefited Men of Color. Both left out Women of Color. Intersectional models speak to the compounding nature of more than one area of marginalization. Some have also used this idea to highlight how a person can experience oppression, such as sexism, while simultaneously receiving the benefits of white privilege. Because this was not the original intent of Crenshaw's work, we've avoided using this term to describe the intersection we're exploring.[4]

White women in Balance can feel and articulate how the particulars of multiple dimensions of identity lead to people experiencing the world differently. Unlike in the stages of Defense (choosing to focus on sexism) or Projection (choosing to focus on racism), we believe an intersectional analysis strengthens, rather than diffuses, efforts for justice.

So, How Do We Do This?

Many white women want to imagine we are in Balance without having looked deeply at ourselves or increased our knowledge of institutionalized racism and patriarchy. However, there are no short cuts when we've got a lifetime of unlearning to do.

With this in mind, we think it is helpful to have a framework to help guide and remind us of the key components of Balance. Dr. Caprice Hollins adapted a framework of cultural competence from psychologists Drs. Derald and David Sue and activist Judith Katz. She introduced this to Ilsa when they were working together in Seattle Public Schools, and, as Cultures Connecting, they further developed this into a model of social justice together.

The four pillars of Awareness, Knowledge, Skills, and Action/ Advocacy help ground us and build the resilience necessary to sustain our anti-racism practice in the Balance stage. This framework is based on the idea that work for social justice is an ongoing journey, not an event.

FIGURE 8.2.

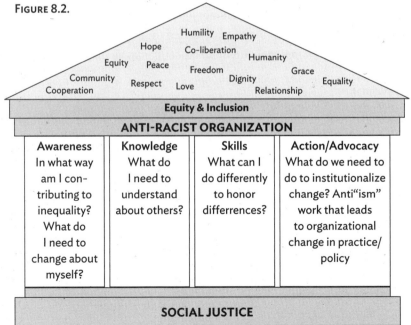

CREDIT: Cultures Connecting, LLC, CulturesConnecting.com

Awareness work involves recognizing one's own racialized and gendered identity, surfacing unconscious bias, and exploring internalized oppression and superiority. *Knowledge* includes understanding cultural differences, institutionalized racism and sexism, and the current and historical social and political context of our communities and interactions. *Skills* to effectively engage within and across cultures are based on self-awareness and knowledge of systems that influence our actions. Because of the complexity of human interactions, memorizing a list of skills without some depth of awareness and knowledge rarely works.

Action and advocacy invoke systems change work. Even as someone might be a good, *non-racist* person, true change involves *anti-racist* policies and practices. In other words, changing institutional and structural racism must coincide with personal growth. This model assumes that cultural differences are not problematic, that oppression comes from the structures and institutions that uphold wealthy, white, male, able-bodied, Christian, and heterosexual supremacy.

We've used the stories from the focus groups and our own lives to illustrate how shifts in our awareness, knowledge, skills, and action and advocacy made it possible to advance toward a more liberated way of treating ourselves and others. Because many of us have so few examples of what Balance can look like in our everyday lives, we deliberately include more stories in this chapter.

Awareness

"[People who strive for social justice are] actively in the process of becoming aware of [their] own assumptions about human behavior, values, biases, preconceived notions, personal limitations, and so forth."[5]

White women's experiences with sexism can serve to further divide us from People of Color until we get what we feel we deserve or our experiences can provide insight for us to empathize with people who are also oppressed. If we don't recognize and heal our oppression and resulting trauma, we are less likely to empathize with others.

In Balance, the rules of being a good ally are not as important as strengthening our awareness of self and understanding the context of our interactions. Having the foundation that allows for more awareness during real-time situations allows white women to respond in more imaginative, authentic, and nimble ways.

As we move into Balance, we begin to realize the "rules of allyship" we have taken care to learn in Projection conflict with one another. For example, I'm not supposed to cry, but I'm not supposed to be disconnected from my heart. I can't make mistakes, but I have to be open to new learning. I'm supposed to follow the lead of People of Color, but I'm not supposed to expect People of Color to teach me about racism.

In Balance, the dualism is reconciled as we become more comfortable in the ambiguous zones beyond righteousness and live into the hazy areas between the poles.

The Smallness of the Bigness We Live

Ilsa related a story from her experience at the Social Justice Training Institute (SJTI), a four-day intensive facilitated by Vernon A. Wall, Dr. Kathy Obear, Rev. Dr. Jamie Washington, and becky martinez.

> In a large multicultural group on our second day together, I was sharing a dynamic I'd seen us white people doing that I thought reflected how messed up we were around our privilege. A Woman of Color responded by stating forcefully, "What do you want, a gold star?" She then went on to talk about many of the problems with white people in this group who saw themselves as allies. It took every ounce of my understanding to not react immediately with, "That's not what I meant!" Instead, I listened to her and others talk about their experiences with white people.
>
> After many tears shed in the white caucus and my hotel room, as well as sleepless nights, I was able to really digest where she was coming from and the fact that she saw something real in me I had not seen in myself. I later apologized

to the group for my impact, without trying to fix the story of how I wanted them to see me. This doesn't mean I didn't care. I desperately wanted everyone to like me and see my goodness. But *I* wasn't the point.

What makes this an illustration of Balance is how Ilsa noticed her reaction internally (awareness), then intentionally chose not to respond right away. She processed emotions in her room and in a white caucus, rather than expecting everyone to spend more time on her experience in the multicultural group. In the end, she realized that trying to control how others saw her was a futile exercise and not one that centered justice.

As Jessica pointed out in a conversation, this is a stage where we recognize the "smallness of the bigness we live."

She spoke about making a public comment in a room of about sixty people where, in trying to connect with a Black male friend of hers, she unintentionally minimized him. He responded by saying as much in front of the group. Immediately she thought, "Do not cry. Do not fix." As the facilitator called for a lunch break, she sat in the discomfort and waited to see if he wanted to reach out to her, rather than approach him to try to make herself feel better. When he did come over to her, they talked and hugged, both affirming the goodness they saw in one another, while not trying to rewrite or backtrack around what had happened and the hurt it caused him.

Although the moment felt huge to her, she realized some people didn't notice what had happened or accepted it and moved on in their learning. While the experience was all *she* could think about, in all that was happening with everyone else, it was a small moment for the group as a whole.

Ilsa remembers coming to this same realization at SJTI, where she processed and cried over all the moments that were huge for her yet, in talking with others in the group, realized they were similarly focused on their own moments. The leap between Projection and Balance involves de-centering oneself.

You're So in Your Body

As we spoke about Balance with the focus group in Seattle, we worked to co-create a definition for this phase. Mallory seemed to capture the essence of self-awareness when she shared,

> I don't feel the need to explain my intent, even though I know it might have been missed...And I really care more about the impact on that person. It's not that you're not in your body; you're so in your body. You're not worried that much about you, and what's going to happen to you, and how everybody sees you, but instead you're really able to just sit with the impact and that person's experience and be with them.
>
> So, it feels to me like...all of the constant things that people [do]...the self-doubt, just kind of calms and settles and we're just able to be really, really present with whatever that situation is. Either...the everything of it—or that one person that I'm impacting—of it. And having a real kind of authentic interchange or just connectedness with the world.

Katy added to this and wondered,

> If I'm noticing it, then I'm living...as Balanced as my maturity will allow me to be...
>
> "Oh, I'm feeling like I want to be a good white person right now. Oh, am I looking at the Person of Color because I'm talking about People of Color? Is that happening right now?"
>
> So, I think maybe Balance is this group. This is Balance when we are having the conversation...I can still be noticing that I'm worried about how people think of me but being in Balance [means]...I'm not going to be reactive about it.

The stories above highlight the value of noticing oneself as a skill set. Without awareness, we might immediately react, as illustrated in earlier phases of development.

Christine added another example that demonstrates reflection on her physical awareness in Balance.

One of the ways that I realized that my internalized op-pression was actually preventing me from seeing the way that my privilege was playing out actually had to do with my physical body…Because of my internalized oppression I have only, for the most part, experienced my body as a point of shame. You know…and the objectification. And my experience with men like, focusing on parts of my body and feeling completely free to say things and do things, and so all of that I internalized, and carried a lot of…shame of my body and…a lot of times just kind of erased it from my consciousness.

It was actually here at WPC (White Privilege Confer-ence) I went to a workshop, and it was super crowded, and we're all sitting like super close to each other. And I was… into the speaker so I was just kind of, like, paying attention. And this Black woman next to me finally tapped me and said, "Would you please stop touching me."

I hadn't even realized that I was touching her, but I could tell from the way she shared it that I was clearly upsetting her. And so, I said I was sorry and she…said, "Okay."

Then I took another deep breath and I said, "I want to thank you because I have never thought before about my body, like my actual physical presence being able to exert white power, white supremacy, white privilege because of my internalized oppression." And if she hadn't said it to me, I would never have known. And now because of that, I re-alized how much undoing my internalized oppression was necessary for me to even be able to see some of the ways that I operate from a place of privilege and whiteness.

Christine had to simultaneously acknowledge that she had inter-nalized sexist messages to make herself small and messages that she was entitled to space. Many People of Color have spoken to us about the amount of emotional, intellectual, and physical space white people take up. Connecting this to internalized sexism allows us to reflect more deeply on and, therefore, address the root causes of our behavior. In this example, the feedback (received graciously) opened a door of awareness to not just taking up space but a litany of other behaviors at the intersection of sexism and white privilege.

Christine and the other white women we spoke with recognize the awareness pillar as deeply valuable in their everyday social justice practice. Unlike the phase we call Projection, in which we want to do something to move out of our guilt as quickly as possible, white women in Balance linger here. *How we are* becomes as meaningful as *what we do*.

Knowledge

People who strive for social justice attempt to understand the worldview of culturally diverse populations. They seek to learn about the values, assumptions, practices, communication styles, group norms, biases, experiences of marginalization, perspectives, and so on, of culturally diverse clients, colleagues, and communities. They commit themselves to learn more about the historical and current social and political context of racism both locally and globally.

The cultivation of seeds of knowledge in earlier phases provides our roots in Balance. It is while in this phase that we are actively applying and practicing that knowledge. This doesn't mean understanding is easy and straightforward. As Michael Eric Dyson reminds us in *Tears We Cannot Stop*, "Beloved truth is rarely neat. It is often messy. Black truth in white America is especially inconvenient."[6]

Part of being in Balance is continually and deliberately learning about theories and stories from people who have researched, lived, and reflected on the topics of sexism and white privilege, particularly People of Color.

These ideas and theories are not new. As discussed in the Capitulation chapter, People of Color have pointed out the connection between these two phenomena for hundreds of years. Angela Davis analyzed these dynamics with precision in 1983 in her book, *Women, Race, and Class.* The key to gaining this knowledge is first to be open to finding it, second to be open to reading, watching, and listening to it, and third and most importantly, to believe what is expressed, especially when shared by People of Color.

There is a dissonance that can occur when learning about new perspectives. Some of them feel like they challenge the core of our morality in a system where our goodness is so closely tied to our privilege. This is when we must be disciplined about "installing the alternative software" that Peggy McIntosh describes, to not default to wanting to feel comfort over growth. This does not mean we cease to be critical thinkers and/or accept all information we take in. Rather, it means we deliberately retain a disposition of curiosity and awareness when feeling challenged.

In the book *Soy Bilingüe: Adult Dual Language Model*, Tilman highlights these five areas of knowledge white people will benefit from exploring:

1. Learn and know our history of racial, class, and linguistic oppression, as well as examples of people similarly privileged who chose a path of resistance.
2. Learn and understand who we are as cultural beings.
3. Learn and understand our place in the United States power structure.
4. Read as many books and articles as possible by People of Color. Watch as many videos and listen to audio recordings of People of Color to develop a deeper and wider understanding of non-white lives.
5. Become familiar with how and why the concept of whiteness was born.[7]

In Balance, we need to learn more about our cultural, political, and familial histories. This exercise helps white women to understand that our liberation depends on all people's liberation. Chris described discovering the cost of white privilege in her family's story.

There's this place and it's about structural understanding. And I think I can spend a fair amount of time there the more I understand about history and the structures that I move in every day. It's a place where it's absolutely impossible for me to feel guilty because I am in a state of mourning, because I understand the costs of dehumanization on every single level. Very importantly I understand, feel, can see, and am living the cost of the dehumanization...It's almost like it feels inappropriate at certain stages to talk about it as privilege...I can see what it takes to have that power, right? That easy access and that smoothness is a kind of disconnection that actually kills you. And I can see how it kills you, and I can feel how it kills you, and I can feel how it's killing me, and I can see how it is literally killing my family members...

[I'm] thinking about Hiroshima and Nagasaki in World War II. When I first learned about the atomic bombs dropped on those cities, it felt really shocking, really far from me...and just horrifying guilt that we did that to them. Then I learned about how Native tribes in Alaska were digging for the uranium [for the bombs], and a lot of people in Alaska died of cancer from digging for the uranium...They were not told how this uranium would be used. It's more complex than just we, America, did this to you, Japan, far away.

My aunt died a couple of years ago of this mysterious thyroid related disorder. She died alone in the bathroom. She had locked herself in. She was pretty young. My other aunt has a big scar like someone slit her throat because when she was thirteen they removed her thyroid glands... And my mom hasn't slept for probably five years for more than two hours and when you see her, she's just a body of pain. She's always told me from the time that I was very young that in our family we have thyroid problems and it's genetic, and I didn't really take her seriously. I just thought, maybe we do and it's just genetic, and it's like the gods decided.

I have this passionate pursuit of understanding inequity in this country. So, in my free time, I read all these books that will tell me these horrible stories which will help me understand more about the structures of inequality. I was reading James Loewen's book about monuments across the United States. I opened up to this page and it described the monument in Mercury, Nevada, which is not too many miles away from where my mom was born in Ogden, Utah. Mercury, Nevada is a testing site where the United States released, I believe it was [many times] the amount of radiation released, at Chernobyl. From a period between 1952, and I believe the last above-ground explosions ended in the seventies, but then they had below ground explosions all the way until 1992.[8]

Then I remembered my mom telling me when she was very young, they used to play in the gray fallouts because they lived on an air force base. She thought she was more protected because they made them stay inside because they were very young. But she remembered the sister who died—would go out because it was curious and interesting.

And just reading it I called my mom and I said, "Mom, this place Mercury, Nevada, did you know about this?" And she said, "No. I didn't know about that."

I'm thinking about my own health and how this is passed on. I have hypothyroidism. I cannot get warm. Sometimes my temperature is 94.9 degrees…I can feel how sick my body is at such a young age. And then I feel on such a profound level how ridiculous it is for me to think that I'm so distant from these people in Nagasaki and Hiroshima, who have atomic bomb illness because there is no way that we could have done that to them and not be touched by it in some horrific way like this. And then I can see how closely it's all connected. This kind of harm cannot be done without it reverberating in everyone's life.

And when I can understand that, it's a place beyond guilt. It's a place of such deep understanding where I can see in my own life…My mom is really sick; and my aunt did die, you know; my dad is really sick. Everything is not going to turn out and [be] okay. Because somehow this grounding and this understanding of how we're all connected to this harm, I just find a lot of peace there. I just feel like, yeah, this is how it goes sometimes. It's not okay, it's just not okay and this touches all of us…

If one group of people is going to treat another group of people like that, you can't believe that's just going to be isolated to that group of people. No, they are going to treat their own children that way. Because then it becomes a pattern of relation that is endemic…Yeah, you can get a promotion and you can have all this money and power and people believing in you and you can be the ideal…What does it mean if you have so much power?

I can actually sit and think, What does it mean to be Bill Gates? I can't imagine the immense inability to connect with other people when you have that much power. Are people really going to be honest with you? Are they going to tell you how they feel because you have so much power over them? I can just see so clearly that power over other people does not allow for power within, to connect with other people. They're mutually exclusive. When you're exercising power over, you cannot exercise power within. And the more you have power over, and the more you've been given power over, not of your choosing, the harder it is for you to connect and feel what other people feel.

It's almost like it's connected to continually trying to believe in the good of this society and trying to do the right thing and follow the laws and work hard the way you're supposed to. And I think often times when we do that it leads us into a place that's really hard because this society is built on so much violence. And I think it's just really violent for all of us.

As she was sharing, Chris began crying, mourning the many interconnected losses. She brilliantly illustrates the amount of time she spends trying to understand and analyze inequity and the many linked pieces of our history she wasn't taught in school. Her tears and her story demonstrate how the intellectual pursuits and foundation that make Balance possible will simultaneously be felt deeply and personally.

Skills

"[People who strive for social justice are] in the process of actively developing and practicing appropriate, relevant, and sensitive strategies and skills in working with culturally diverse clients, families, communities and colleagues."[9]

Awareness and knowledge in and of themselves often lead to a change in behaviors. Robin reflected on how internally challenging the messages she'd got that she was less than because of her gender and class, led to the action of voicing opposition to white privilege. "I had to say it's a lie that you are not as smart as anybody else here [at the University]. It's a lie that you don't belong here. So, when you speak up [against racism] you are simultaneously challenging the lie of your internalized sexism and class oppression and speaking up against white privilege. So, for me, it's just been a profoundly powerful way to address both internalized oppression and internalized white superiority."

However, awareness and knowledge don't guarantee skillful actions. White women must apply the skills we learn continually; not only when it is expected or convenient.

While in the stage we call Projection, white women may feel frozen when trying to engage with Black men. In Balance, we practice the skills of engaging in ways that recognize our complex, interconnected histories. Ilsa recalls taking the risk to interrupt a Black man who had spoken three times already in a large-group workshop. She thanked him and pointed out how much she appreciated what he'd added to the conversation, then asked if he would make space for others to share their ideas, given we only had a short amount of time together. He responded by becoming upset with her and shutting down. In that moment, Ilsa felt she had made the right decision in prioritizing the needs of the larger group over her fear of being seen as racist. She later reflected on how their interaction resulted from a lifetime of experiences they each brought to that one moment. He saved face and reclaimed power by declaring, "Fine, I just won't speak anymore." In Balance, white women can better recognize how a Person of Color's reaction may simultaneously be about us and not about us.

Laura spoke about the challenge of navigating power dynamics as a white woman married to a Black man.

> We'll be in situations where I know my white privilege is going to play out. So, the restaurant looks full. You wait out here and I'm going to go in and deal with it. That's a very common situation, but there are other situations where I'm going to handle things because I'm white, which traditionally the male would handle…Just that emasculating of my husband, who I love to death and who doesn't agree with white privilege, and so I just think how painful is that for him when he loves to take care of me and our family and then he has to do that? Or in front of my family or even in front of our son, has to say, "I need you to go deal with that." I just think it's really, really painful.

The traditional Eurocentric definition of "masculinity," the man as the caretaker, implies a woman should be less powerful. Keenly aware of how to utilize white privilege to their advantage, Laura's family also must live with the perceptions of the outside world that her husband cannot, at times, live up to what it means to be a man. The expectations of structural sexism collide with racist stereotypes, and together they must navigate this in their family.

The goal is not perfection. In the stage we call Balance, we have learned enough that we can adjust our responses and interactions with people, take chances, and see missteps as integral to progress. We recognize that our interactions happen within the context of our history, and each individual brings different experiences and levels of personal awareness and knowledge to those interactions. We must be willing to try to interfere with sexism and white supremacy and then learn from our successes, challenges, and outright failures.

Wrestling Together

Terrie shared a story about how she creatively used skills in a work setting.

> I was on a planning committee for a retreat. We had a facilitator who we really honor and respect. And when we were talking about how we were going to open [the retreat], she said, "I have this great tool and I know you folks are going to just love it. It's a [Lakota] Native American Medicine Wheel. It was adapted to be an exercise to help people take a look at their strengths and abilities/challenges and looking and identifying in what part of the wheel they would fall."
>
> Well, we loved it because people identified with animals. [The exercise] generated really good talk, and we were a mixed group, Pacific Islanders, Latinx, Somali, and people who have Indigenous backgrounds, maybe not Lakota.
>
> But we had this experience and it really, really opens up the day, and we were really engaged in it. The deer were looking at their processing, and the buffaloes are looking at the way they just bulldoze through things, and the eagles are talking about getting the big picture, and it helped kind of get an understanding of each other.
>
> So, we come back to [work] and someone hears that we did this and pointed out how it was a very serious act of appropriating someone else's culture. They were very of-

fended. And other people in the group said, "Oh, it sort of triggered me too, but I didn't say anything."

And I sat in that meeting and I went through every phase of Defense and Projection. Like from going, "Well my culture's being appropriated all the time."

I get it, and I don't know why I didn't see it, but I wasn't feeling it. I was trying to figure out why I [didn't feel it]. Am I so in Defense that I'm not feeling it? What is going on?

I think where I'm talking about Balance is that I finally got to the point where I could have a conversation with other people without feeling the necessity to feel so bad. To feel so guilty. To feel the tears coming on. To feel like I should have said something; I should have caught it.

Because I realized that in that moment, I'm just so excited that [we participated] in something, and it was exposed. I was like, "Oh Wow! Now I'm going to hope that we fucking learn something from this experience. I mean I'm going to think about it. I'm going to think about it in a group."

I know that I wasn't denying that we appropriated this, but I was also feeling like I could say more than, "I feel so sorry. I'm so embarrassed. I'm feeling so ashamed." That I could also say, "What a great opportunity that we actually [exposed this]."

The learning just went on, and on, and on. And somehow in there, even though I was experiencing defensiveness and projections, there was this sense of every now and then, you know, shifting. I felt a little Balance in there. And, it's memorable. I accepted the dissonance.

In Terrie's example, she doesn't try to make anyone the enemy to blame, including herself. Instead, she wonders about the facilitator's story as well as her coworkers' experiences. They work collectively to get as much learning out of their misstep of cultural appropriation as possible.

Off-Balance is Balance

Ilsa shared an illustration of the deliberate decisions involved as a white woman practicing anti-racism skills.

> I was facilitating a meeting with about forty people on an Equity Team, a group purposed with changing policies and practices in schools that create opportunity gaps. In the room were diverse community members and staff representing a variety of stakeholders. The district leadership showed a video that negatively impacted many in the room. As I tried to navigate the emotions, race and gender dynamics, organizational hierarchy, and a variety of opinions, I felt unsure. Off-balance.
>
> There were a few things clear in my mind: stay with and normalize the emotions; invite feedback on the impact and redirect from intention; own it as if it were my idea to show the video rather than avoid responsibility; slow down and listen carefully; and be ready to scrap the agenda.
>
> However, I had no idea where the conversation was going to take us and felt extremely uncomfortable. As the one holding the space, would I be able to prioritize justice and the needs of the group? What if those conflicted?
>
> The fact that I, as a white woman, felt off-kilter indicated that my white cultural norms for meetings were not central. Stretching into the zone of discomfort and listening as if my life depended on it to the voices of People of Color allowed us all to move forward together to a different definition of "forward" than I had at the start of the meeting.
>
> I actively facilitated—redirecting, questioning, paraphrasing, connecting—rather than shying away from my role out of guilt or my white superiority. And I tried to balance this with good "followership" of People of Color most impacted by the video.

Ironically, this sense of imbalance is an indicator of Balance. The de-centering of whiteness naturally causes white people to feel uncertainty, as we rarely inhabit a space where our norms, desires, opinions, questions, agendas, etc. don't reign supreme.

Collecting Our People

People of Color have repeatedly called on white people to educate each other about our privilege. Mallory illustrated the important skill of seeking connection with white people that is characteristic of Balance. She spoke about a white colleague she had a long history with and "pretty much detested at that point."

> It was another barrier that she was trying to throw up, and I was getting ready to say something horrible to her about who she was. I stopped and instead asked her questions: "Why is that important to you? And why is *that* important to you? And then why is *that* important to you?"
>
> And pretty soon she had tears in her eyes, and she was talking about her experiences growing up with no money, in single-parent household, and how now it's hard for her to not be reliving those experiences because she is a single mother with adopted children...Even sharing she's worried that she shouldn't have adopted and is she a good adoptive mother?
>
> I wasn't really focusing on myself at all. I wasn't trying to be a good white person...There were all kinds of people in the room—white people, People of Color, people with working-class backgrounds, people of privilege, and everything in between. I wasn't thinking about how I was coming across to them. I was actually really focused on her, and what was alive in her, and why she was being the person that she was.
>
> And...I could imagine that it would often follow that because she was seen, and because I cared about her in that conversation and wanted to know and had curiosity, she was no longer a barrier for us to do what we needed to do...I get little glimpses of things in experiences like that, and what they have in common is that I'm not the center of it. I'm curious about other people. I'm not worried about, "Do I look good?"

In Projection, we falsely believe looking good as a social justice advocate means being hard enough on other white people. We might worry that others in the room will think we are friends with the "problematic" white person and, therefore, share all of the same beliefs. Letting go of this need to be seen as an ally allows white women to better act as accomplices for justice. As in Mallory's story, we connect, rather than assert our superiority. In so doing, we act in more liberating ways for all people.

Christine reflected on how deliberately using skills helped her to work collaboratively with white men instead of fighting them.

> So, back when I realized I needed to find a way to heal myself so that I could reach out to white men with love and compassion, that [is what] changed my practice. And that has changed [me] immensely as a facilitator.
>
> It was in a workshop in the summer where I was finally...ready to try it, and I worked with three different white men and just being mindful and curious about their experience and their pain. And it was the first time that I ever really actually believed and saw white men's pain around racism. Because I had never entertained that they would experience that. And it was internalized oppression that had prevented that. And now I feel like I can be more effective in actually fighting racism which wasn't what I was doing before. Because I can meet white men and try to join with them rather than fighting with them.

Although we may push away from other white women because we don't want to be seen as similar to them, connecting with white men in work for justice can be even more challenging. Our past experiences with sexism may have equipped us with healthy wariness. Just as white people will inevitably act out our superiority with People of Color, white men will inevitably demonstrate paternalistic behaviors. White women in Balance remind ourselves of the socialization that created these actions. While this doesn't excuse microaggressions, it does mean we approach other white people as potential change agents and not as the enemy.

Circling Back: A Mistake and A Repair

A part of being in Balance means recognizing we will mess up and continue to mess up and knowing that when we do, we may lose friends and coworkers as a result. Katy spoke about how she messed up with a Black coworker, made amends, and their resulting conversation.

There's a woman who is in an adjacent department…She was a relatively new staff member a few months ago…I'm a supervisor in my department, so a slight bit of power above in that hierarchical way, but we don't work together…One day, we're passing each other in the hallway, and I said, "Oh, you look very elegant today. Your hair is different. You look very elegant."

And she said in a very confident tone with a little bit of edge, "You know, I look elegant every day. I just dried my hair straight today."

Right? And so, I said, "You know you're absolutely right. You look fabulous every day." So that was the interaction.

A few weeks later I went up to her and I said, "Is this a good time? Do you have five or ten minutes? I wanted to talk to you."

And she said, "Sure."

"You know, I just wanted to apologize about the impact of my statement about you. And I know that hair is a very loaded topic. I'm aware of surface positive intentions I had and other unconscious, you know, boxes I put you in. I have a privilege in that area. I guess I just want to acknowledge that, and I really loved your response. It really heightened my awareness and I just really appreciate it."

She was very lovely in her response. "Thank you so much." And she had this whole story that I didn't know, and so we had an interaction where I felt I did some cleanup.

She found me again in the hallway another month or two later and said, "Hey do you have twenty minutes or so? I'd love to talk to you."

So we grabbed a space, and she just said, "You know, I've been wanting to talk to you because…I've seen in a few interactions I've had with you, I have felt like you kind of exemplify some of the things…[I appreciate]."

When she was all done, I just said, " I love the concept and I'm proud to be walking some of the walk. I don't even know the number of times that I got it wrong that you didn't see, and on whose backs and shoulders I learned so that I came back to you about the hair. How many times did I say something like that and didn't catch it, didn't acknowledge my injury, so that I could acknowledge an injury with you and have this positive impact."

I didn't feel like I was doing that to be humble. "You just haven't seen how many times I've done it. It was still a mistake and a repair. There were so many mistakes I didn't repair because I didn't know any better, or I was afraid to say something, or who knows what. And so, I'm going to acknowledge that it had a positive impact on you, and that's wonderful. And I have to be honest with the fact that there are so many other people that didn't get that."

I felt like in that moment of, like, thank you and you've just missed all the other times. And it's going to end. I hope that when I mess up with you again, because I will, and I won't catch it, that you'll feel comfortable letting me know. I'm glad that so far, we're okay, but I'm feeling a little bit like by the grace of "whatever" I've got to this place. I'm sure you will see me trip and fall, and I hope we will have built enough relationship that you'll be able to tell me. Because it's the only way I've got where I've got, which I'm not saying is that far. So that was my moment of Balance.

In this example of Balance, Katy recognizes all the practice it took to get to the point of being able to own her impact, and her coworker graciously accepts her apology. Katy notes the likelihood that she will make more mistakes in the future, and she doesn't try to prove she is better than her white colleagues, even when her Black coworker saw her as different.

Balance involves moving beyond the guilt of our mistakes and seeing how we learn and grow from those experiences. We acknowledge that racism and sexism are structural and deeply embedded in our society and our personhood. As Terrie made a point of telling us, it shouldn't and doesn't surprise us when we mess up.

Circling back is a powerful strategy, even after quite a bit of time has passed. In our workshops and workplaces, we frequently hear white women talking about an incident with a Person of Color where they now realize they messed up. But, they say, it was a while ago and I don't know if the person even remembers. Or it might make it worse if I say something now. Or I'm sure that Person of Color just wants to move on with their life and not have to relive this moment I've been agonizing over. Usually, the real reason is taking the risk to apologize makes us uncomfortable.

We also frequently hear People of Color talking about a white woman coworker who said or did something racist a while ago, and she still hasn't apologized. Or she just went on as if nothing had happened.

The risk of causing more harm to People of Color by not repairing damage runs much deeper than the possible damage of the repair itself. Sometimes the person will have forgotten the incident altogether, and sometimes it will make it worse. However, the apology shows genuine care and accountability for our actions. It is better to be held accountable for what we have done, rather than what we've failed to do.

Tilman shared an example of a repair after much time had passed.

A couple of years before, in the name of "humor," I had insulted a friend in a very public setting. He let me know immediately that I had been insensitive and racist. The incident lasted maybe thirty seconds, but I had always held this moment in my mind and heart, and in spite of seeing my friend many times since, I had never apologized. I rationalized that we weren't close enough, or that it had happened so far in the past, or that he wouldn't want me to bring it up again. And, interestingly, even though I talked about moments like these regularly within caucuses and with colleagues and friends, I had never shared this particular one with anyone. It wasn't until I was writing this book that I finally shared the story out loud and fully realized how deeply disrespectful I had been. This was someone I admired and cared about, so there was no reason to not apologize.

My defensiveness did not warrant protecting my ego from the guilt I felt at being so insensitive. The only way to move forward with integrity and to heal was to own my behavior. So, after almost a year, I did send an apology to my friend, sending it late and wording it imperfectly. But the point was not that I could or should do this perfectly or seek his forgiveness in some way; the point was that I did it.

Action/Advocacy

Somewhere there is a skillful white demagogue becoming aware of how effortlessly he could exploit white fear and convince the white majority it is "necessary" to intern those we fear.
He could persuade us easily to trade our morality and our freedoms for our "safety" and his power...The wall between two groups of Americans was built with millions of stones and I have finally come to believe it can only be removed by millions of white people each taking one stone away.

— Lois Mark Stalve, *The Education of a WASP*

As we take action and advocate in Balance, each taking away a stone, we must know our history and remain vigilant in recognizing how often white women have acted "on behalf of" People of Color, only to capitulate to our feelings of gender oppression or the allure of white power. As discussed earlier, examples of this include but are not limited to Elizabeth Cady Stanton and Susan B. Anthony trading in their anti-slavery effort chips to win (white) female suffrage; the Feminist movement of the '70s that ultimately turned its back on the voices and leadership of Women of Color; and the majority of teachers in this country, white women who seem consigned to not change a system that is funneling young Boys and Girls of Color toward prison. We must remember what Ruth Frankenberg wrote in *The Social Construction of Whiteness: White Women, Race Matters*: "Racism was and is something that shapes white women's lives, rather than something that People of Color have to live and deal with in a way that bears no relationship or relevance to the lives of white people."[10] In other words, our actions to transform our society must be with, rather than to or for, People of Color.

Developing the mindset and skills of Balance can positively impact relationships in our homes, our communities, and our workplaces, hopefully creating more equitable and compassionate environments and opportunities for all of us. We mustn't rest there, however. While there are positive outcomes from working on our individual interactions, the parallel goal must be to go beyond our individual practices to impact institutions and systems that inequitably favor white men.

Most of the women we interviewed identify as activists. They are advocating through teaching, performing, engaging in creative arts, publishing books, protesting in the streets, testifying to local officials, and changing laws in Washington, DC. They address institutional policies as social workers, educators, consultants, parents, and facilitators. Each has found her place in a movement for justice based on her talents, interests, and circle of influence. This changes and morphs over time. In other words, there are myriad paths for collective action.

Final Thoughts

Although this chapter contains many stories and strategies, moving to Balance doesn't involve replicating a model, it takes time and energy. White women must choose every day to unlearn what we've been taught about our race and gender, gain a deeper understanding of racist and patriarchal systems, and prioritize speaking up at the expense of our comfort. Despite the potential consequences, we take the risks for the rewards of our collective freedom.

When we move from the external to the internal and build the foundational skills where all of our education, reading, experiences, and strategies come into play, this creates the conditions for moments of Integration, the next stage, to occur.

Despite the seriousness and challenges of oppression, we stay in Balance more often when we laugh together and encourage one another. As anarchist Emma Goldman said in 1931, "I want freedom, the right to self-expression, everybody's right to beautiful, radiant things...A revolution without dancing is not a revolution worth having."[11]

Feeling Balance

Stretch your arms out to either side, palms facing up. Rock gently back and forth, feeling the tension of nearly tipping, before catching yourself. If you can, rock from one foot to the other. Move around carefully considering your direction and making intentional decisions of where you will go, all the while continuing to rock from side to side.

As you encounter other people, indicate with your body language an invitation for them to join you or an interest in joining with them. See if you can synchronize your movements with one another. Look fully and take in the details of people's physical and emotional presence. Notice who is easy for you to connect with and who is more difficult for you.

- As you held this gesture, what felt natural to you? What felt unnatural?
- What feelings came up for you? Where did these feelings land in your body?
- If you were with other women when you tried this gesture, how did their bodies feel and look to you? How did you feel toward them?
- How did this feel similar to and different from the other gestures?

Strategic Questions for Balance

- Describe a time that you have been in Balance. How did it feel? Who was there? What did it sound like?
- What specific/concrete steps help you to get to Balance and stay there?
- What keeps you from being in Balance? What could prompt you to return to Immersion, Capitulation, Defense, or Projection?
- Talk about another white woman you've seen acting in Balance. What stood out about her?
- How are your relationships with People of Color different when you are in Balance versus earlier phases?
- In what ways are you working to increase your self-awareness?
- What new knowledge are you pursuing?
- How are your practicing your anti-racism skills?
- In what ways are you advocating for systemic changes that promote justice?

9

Integration

One of the extraordinary things about liberation is that
you do not feel the need to control things when you're free,
because the illusory nature of control becomes clear to you.

— Rev. angel Kyodo williams

TRY TO REMEMBER a time when you were in active community and collaboration with a group, whether it was singing
in a choir, playing in a band, competing in a team sport, building
a structure, or chanting/praying. Remember an instant when you
forgot where you were or what you were doing and were simultaneously fully present in what was happening and unaware you
were so focused. In these moments, there is a sense of together-
ness and presence that transcends intentional thought.

This connection, however fleeting, is what we are calling
Integration. We chose this name because it means separate parts
coming together to become a whole altogether different than the
individual components. We think of this as integrating our understanding of sexism and racism into a new way of being. White
women in this phase simultaneously recognize the connections
between personal, cultural, institutional, and structural oppression and privilege.

For white women in the phase of Integration, understanding, identifying, and living with the intersections of white supremacy and sexism is a way of being rather than just knowing.
When we're experiencing Integration, it is not something we're
doing, it's everything we're doing. We have a sense of our com-

mon humanity while holding our vast differences and the reality of structures that divide us. This is different from Balance in that there are fewer, or no, strategies being carefully navigated. It also should not be confused with a "color-blind" type of love where our differences don't matter. Rather, having historic and current knowledge of systems of oppression makes the space for deeper connections within and across our differences. Integration involves experiences, moments in time, when our values, beliefs, and actions are aligned.

In Integration, white women acknowledge our pain to heal internalized sexism and white privilege without using it to excuse, minimize, or justify racism. This idea is captured by anti-racist activist Valerie Kaur in her TED talk about revolutionary love when she outlines three ways of being that are core pieces to what we are calling Integration.

> Number one: In order to love others, see no stranger. We can train our eyes to look upon strangers on the street, on the subway, on the screen, and say in our minds, "Brother, sister, aunt, uncle, [sibling]." And when we say this, what we are saying is, "You are a part of me I do not yet know. I choose to wonder about you."

We identify this as empathy.

> Number two: In order to love our opponents, tend the wound. Can you see the wound in the ones who hurt you? Can you wonder even about them? But remember…Loving our opponents requires us to love ourselves. Gandhi, King, Mandela—they taught a lot about how to love others and opponents. They didn't talk a lot about loving ourselves. This is a feminist intervention.

We identify this as self-love.

> Number three: In order to love ourselves, breathe and push. When we are pushing into the fires in our bodies or the fires in the world, we need to be breathing together in

order to be pushing together. How are you breathing each day? Who are you breathing with? How are you protecting your joy each day? Because in joy we see even darkness with new eyes.

We identify this as self-care.

As Kaur points out in her talk, these organic practices of empathy, self-love, and self-care create the foundation or conditions for moments of Integration. If we are judgmental, self-shaming, and/or spread too thin, we will not have the capacity to address patriarchy and white supremacy either proactively or reactively.[1]

Capturing a Moment

In the two-day workshop we facilitate, we have an activity for this phase to illustrate how Integration works and feels. We teach the participants the words to a simple song and then have them sing it in a round, a style where different groups start singing at different times and may continue indefinitely. Most people in the United States are familiar with singing a round to the song "Row, Row, Row Your Boat."

We teach a children's song in our workshops that is comprised of sounds ("Ram, Sam, Sam"). We split the group into equal sections of five to ten women. We then ask each group to participate in the round with one of us conducting. Participants are having to remember the words and tune; stay in sync with their section; pay attention to the other groups; and pay attention to the conductor. By the time they sing the song three or four times, they begin to flow more easily. By the time they reach six or seven rounds, they are pretty much in sync and can hear and feel the room around them. When it comes to an end, most participants, even those who claim they can't sing or found the activity goofy at first, recognize they all played a part in creating a beautiful sound and experience.

We then ask the group how they are feeling, and what they just experienced. The descriptors often are words like *connected, present, integrated, still in time, aligned*—all words we think of as illustrative of Integration. One woman stated, "I was aware of my voice and how I harmonized with the women in my section and of the sound of the larger group and how the same melody connected us, even as we were singing different parts." These three levels can be seen to represent the personal, cultural, and systemic, all experienced simultaneously. The key to this activity is to get us out of our heads and fully into our other senses, focused and receptive, so we can experience the sensation of Integration.

Katy talked about all of the hard work in Balance necessary to have a moment of Integration.

> I think Integration is hard for me to remember in the same way that joy is hard to remember. Like in the moment when I'm sitting with my family and then I go, "I am happy. This is what happy feels like." And then boom it's gone. The minute you try to capture that air it's not there anymore. In the moment, I can't even remember what that feels like because to know what it feels like means to try and stop time that you can't stop.

Chris described a scene from the movie, *Mirrors of Privilege: Making Whiteness Visible*, where Peggy McIntosh talks about creating her list that eventually became the "Unpacking the Invisible Knapsack" article.[2]

> The perfect Balance moment is when Peggy McIntosh describes waking up and then writing down [examples of white privilege], like, "I can buy Band-Aids [designed to match the color of my skin]," and then going back to sleep. It just seems like Balance where you just have this moment of intense clarity where you can see all of the connections. I just love that story where she...kept this thing with paper by her bed.

Katy added, "There is something about keeping it by my bed because I think I might have some insights—that is Balance. The actual moments where she had those insights I think of as Integration. But she created a way for her to have those moments."

Terrie responded, "I'm practicing; I'm practicing; I'm practicing this. I'm going to keep practicing this. Oh, and then that moment when you like don't notice that you're practicing because you got it."

Mallory built on this idea, "I think that is what I was thinking, too. The moment that you wake up, 'Ahh,' that's Integration. It's just all of a sudden, it's there. [It is the opposite of] the practice of saying, 'This is how I'm going to get from here to there, or, 'I'm going to consciously not react,' [instead, it's more like] 'I'm just so with you that I don't even know what my process is.'"

As the women spoke, they overlapped and co-created knowledge together, modeling the very phenomenon they were describing. In their comments, they highlighted how the structure of practice in the Balance phase leads to Integration. They pointed out how we become, if only in that brief moment it takes to forget a dream, unconsciously competent.

Being With One Another

As each of the women in our local focus group discussed their stories of Integration, there was more emotion in the room than on any other night we met. Most of the women cried as they shared and listened to each other. As Chris pointed out, "I feel like I can't touch Integration during those stories that I was sharing without having this strong emotion flow through me. I mean it's like the story *is* emotion."

One of the dynamics of Integration is that a woman moves from the *I* and *me* to *we* and *us*. Our perspective changes long enough to have total empathy for the person or people we are with, and we meet them on an intuitive and heart level as well as an intellectual level.

Terrie described a time sitting with a friend who was dying of cancer:

In that moment I just sat down by her window, and I was staring out at her and seeing all the support she had. I just said, "Wow, this is the sanest I've felt all day." And in that moment, I felt that sense of Integration and things all fitting together the way they were supposed to fit together. Nothing to do. *There wasn't anything to do and I felt so productive.*

Moved by Terrie's example, Mallory added, "Integration is almost like a gift. It's those moments of total awareness and purity or whatever you want to call it."

She shared again about the Somali family in her life:

The pain and agony that human beings have organized for ourselves, that is absolutely true that my country is made out of violence and that's how it got here. But at the same time, I can take [my adopted grandson] off into the woods and show him this beautiful place with running water, green trees with leaves that connect from tree to tree, and all the exciting things about the natural world that excite me so much, the coyote trails and all that. And be absolutely ecstatic about it and have ecstatic experiences. At the same time, remembering [his mother] walking from Somalia to Kenya and lying down along the side of the road to give birth.

So, when I'm able to do that, keeping all of that in mind at once, I'm feeling excited and happy on the verge of those sort of ecstasy feelings. And, at the same time, I feel like crying and low. I feel low and like things will not be okay. And that's where there's no swaying involved. I just feel like I love these people, and many of these people love me, and that's the most important thing. We're going to figure out all the weird, painful hurting things as we go.

The way Mallory describes her experience captures what, in earlier phases, would be felt as contradictory emotions. No longer tied to the either/or binary, feelings naturally overlap with awareness and knowledge, threads in the fabric of Integration.

Terrie shared another example from her life. She talked about working in a domestic violence shelter and the rich connections she had with Women of Color.

There's that kind of Integration. I think it has something to do with some of that revolutionary love and compassion, because we respect the work that each other is doing as parents, as community people, and the individual jobs that we're doing. Then we're all trying to home in on our skills and do the best job for the surviving women in the program.

Trying to be helpful can be such an irritation to other people that perhaps in those moments of [Integration] we all are truly not doing any harm. People get a break from us, or we get a break from ourselves. And there's a lot of relief there.

Up to this point in the model, there is so much effort and energy involved in "doing." As Terrie points out, living with oppression is exhausting; and fighting oppression is exhausting; and dealing with people who are trying to help us in the struggle against oppression is exhausting. She described the work at the shelter as different. It refueled her after a forty-hour workweek.

Integration can happen at any time. In conversations with friends, in our places of work, even when we are alone. Ilsa shared a moment of Integration as a facilitator.

A white woman was having a hard time believing racism still exists, particularly the idea that unintentional micro-aggressions were a problem in today's world. I paused and asked what her experience was with racism. She explained how she had been involved with the civil rights movement and how much she had seen change. After listening carefully (in the literal sense of the word—with care) and asking more questions, I felt a deep sense of empathy with her. I could see her not as defensive or resistant, but as someone who had to give something up to understand what I was saying.

I said to her, "It must be hard to think that after everything you've seen in your lifetime racism is still a problem."

She replied that it was difficult. Pulling from my memory of Lee Mun Wah facilitating in the movie *The Color of Fear*, I then asked, "What would it mean to you if that was the case? If it really was a huge problem still today?"

As she responded, I could hear her voice crack, "It would just be so sad. It would make me so upset."

As she said that, I truly felt with her and saw her shift in considering this could be the case. It was a rare moment of Integration where I invited her to see through a different lens, only after exploring and connecting with where she was at and why. I wasn't trying to convince her. I wasn't using a strategy so much as simply trying to see her story and open a new window for her to look through.

Tilman recognized a similar situation in her facilitation practice. Intentionally pausing, a characteristic of Balance, led to a moment of Integration.

Ilsa and I were facilitating a two-day training for a group of white women who had not voluntarily signed up to participate and who were not necessarily open to the idea that the intersection of internalized sexism and white superiority was an issue for them. There was quite a bit of resistance in the room from several participants, and I had already been triggered once by one of them.

After being triggered, I was concerned about my ability to be open with this group because I was working from a place of Defensiveness and Projection. To try to move toward Balance, during a break I purposely sat down and spent time looking at the faces of these women; trying to imagine who they were, and how this conversation could or could not support their work, and mostly in what ways we were interrelated.

When it was time for us to begin again, a participant shared her pain around her experiences of regularly being confused for a man when at the grocery store and having to deal with sexism, cis-sexism, and homophobia when she just wanted to buy groceries. This woman took a risk in sharing this, and it was a ripe moment for empathy from the group.

Instead, one of the most resistant women spoke up and said, "Oh, come on! Are we really *that* sensitive?"

For whatever reason, in that moment, I was able to turn around and look this woman right in the eye, match her energy and tone, and sincerely say,

"I hear you! This makes you angry, right?!"

"Yes! This makes me angry!" she replied.

Continuing to match her tone, I responded, "But it occurs to me that you're not angry because your coworker feels this way. You're angry because no one ever explained this stuff to you, and in these moments, you feel duped!"

"Yes! That is how I feel! No one ever explained this stuff to me! Why wasn't I taught this? Why am I this age and just learning about it now?!"

This exchange released a lot of tension in the room and brought us together as a collective for a moment. It was fleeting. We had other tense times during our two days together. But this moment of Integration allowed all of us to see one another's humanity and agree that we had all been duped by systemic oppression as white women.

Empathy, compassion, and perspective all played a part in setting up that moment for the group. Normally, Tilman would have been angered and further triggered by what sounded like sarcasm. But the time she had spent trying to imagine what these women were experiencing helped her authentically hear and respond to the woman's anger and despair. She had no thought of, "I'm going to try this strategy and see if it works." She let go of a need to control the direction of the conversation for a moment to be present and feel what the participant felt.

A quote from the Dalai Lama and Desmond Tutu explains this further.

The wider perspective leads to serenity and equanimity. It does not mean we don't have the strength to confront a problem, but we can confront it with creativity and compassion rather than rigidity and reactivity. When we take the perspective of others, we can empathize with them… We are also able to recognize that we do not control all aspects of any situation. This leads to a greater sense of humility, humor, and acceptance.[3]

Final Thoughts

We don't know any white woman who lives the majority of her life in Integration. Perhaps we simply have not met her yet. For this reason, originally the model stopped at Balance. We added Integration as a place to strive for and recognize when we catch glimpses of it out of the corner of our hearts. We're not even entirely sure what we're looking for, and that's okay. We'll know it when we feel it.

Feeling Integration

Sit or stand with both feet on the floor if you are able, in a position where you feel solid and steady. Feel yourself rooted into the ground and light simultaneously. With a partner or in a group, take several deep breaths in and out together. Notice your connection.

- As you held this gesture, what felt natural to you? What felt unnatural?
- What feelings came up for you? Where did these feelings land in your body?
- If you were with other women when you tried this gesture, how did their bodies feel and look to you? How did you feel toward them?
- How did this feel similar to and different from the other gestures?

Strategic Questions for Integration

- Talk about a time when you experienced a moment of Integration. Describe the intersection of sexism and racism that you were experiencing or were responding to. How did you process the awareness of the intersection? Who were you with and what did you do in the moment?
- Describe how moments of Integration have felt for you. How do you know you have had a moment? How do you hold onto the feeling and memory of it?
- What do you do for self-care? How is anti-racism practice organically integrated into your care?
- How are you encouraging and protecting your joy each day? How does embodying this intersection inform your joy?
- How do you play?

10

White Women's Tears

*The legitimate grievances of brown and black women
are no match for the accusations of a white damsel in distress...
white women are equally aware their race privileges them
as surely as ours condemns us. In this context, their tearful
displays are a form of emotional and psychological
violence that reinforce the very system of white dominance
that many white women claim to oppose.*

— Ruby Hamad

IN A RECENT workshop, Ilsa witnessed the power of white women's tears. She shared this story (with names changed).

I was facilitating a workshop in an elementary school where staff had just completed a survey of the ways racism and white privilege show up in their everyday lives. Jill, a white woman, started to explain that because of her class status and growing up in a military family, she'd lived in many communities with People of Color. As I asked questions and pointed out my concern that people in the room would assume she's saying she has the same experience with racism as People of Color, she began to cry. Jill said she didn't know why she was crying. She and another white woman next to her, Jennifer, had never been asked to recognize their privilege. And they'd certainly never been asked to do this in public, in front of their coworkers.

As I asked questions, what another white woman on staff would later call "drilling them," they felt humiliated in front of their peers.

These two white women, who felt put on the spot and believed they were being told they are racist, were worried no one would like them. They cried to elicit sympathy and to regain control. Far from being weak, their tears were a power play.

Jennifer didn't come to work the next day, saying she was too upset. Other white women rallied around them. One gave Jennifer a plant to comfort her.

Instead of looking at the dynamics of white privilege, as intended in the exercise, these women made the experience about individuals. They wrote on feedback forms, "Ilsa doesn't know us and she doesn't know how to lead these conversations. She shouldn't be invited back."

"Jill can believe what she wants. Her life shouldn't be used to make a point about some agenda."

Some staff members got upset that the two women cried at all. They believed the momentary embarrassment Jill and Jennifer felt in being held accountable to recognizing their privilege was akin to living with racism. They said they wanted lesson plans, not to feel guilty about the upheaval racism causes in the lives of People of Color.

Several agreed the exercise we did was great, but they "shut down" when these women were asked questions about their experiences. Therefore, they used that moment to get out of learning more about their white privilege and colluded with racism as a relief to their discomfort.

In the midst of all of this, People of Color on the staff noted that their own emotion was not treated with respect or empathy by other staff members. The tearful stories they shared of the EVERYDAY pain of racism were, in many ways, expected. No one gave them a plant.

This is a point at which conversations about whiteness usually stop in an organization. The "diversity" consultant is not called back. People of Color no longer see the benefit in risking sharing their stories. White women's tears are a powerful force upholding white supremacy.

The act of white women crying and the response to our tears offers a clear example of the intersection of sexism and white privilege and provides a case study of what the same behavior can look like in different stages of our model of anti-racist identity development.

We are not talking about crying in any situation, only those involving racism. Nor are we saying crying is a bad thing. We believe more people should be crying when confronting the ugly truth of racism in the United States. The fact that we don't cry when seeing Latinx children separated from their parents at the border or Black people killed by the police shows a deep disconnection from our shared humanity.

As two white women who tend to cry, we feel it is important to explore why we and other white women cry and the impact our tears have in conversations about racism. We propose there is a connection between a learned behavior that helps us navigate sexism and an assertion of our racial superiority.

Women of Color and Tears

The result is usually quite different when Women of Color cry.

Women of Color's tears have rarely if ever elicited care or support from white men or white women. Educator and activist Anita Garcia Morales wrote in an email correspondence,

> Tears are not a go-to for us to "get our way" or to be seen as "delicate and helpless," because coming from us that is not what they mean, and they would not be interpreted as such by white men because of all they see when they see us (consciously or not). I remember an encounter with a predator as a young woman. He was white…and was invading my private space, which is saying a lot because of my cultural beliefs around that [as a Latina woman]. I had to be firm without an ounce of apology or courtesy and *definitely without giving away any of the harm or minimization* I was

FIGURE 10.1.

Crying Behavior	Individual Responses	Organizational Responses	Impact on People of Color
White woman cries when accused of racism	• Care for her • Reassure her she's innocent • Stop talk about racism • Give her a plant	• Punish the Person of Color accuser • Give minimal or no repercussions to the white woman	• Invalidate and/or ignore experiences of racism • Lose job
Woman of Color cries when talking about racism she experiences	• Question her reality: "Are you sure that was racism?" • Ignore her • See her as weak and overly emotional	• Label her unprofessional • Identify her as having "performance issues"	• Stop speaking up about racism • Develop health issues due to racial stress • Lose job

feeling in the moment. This calls for superhuman powers. We can't feel what we feel because in feeling that we make ourselves a bigger target.[1]

The relationship of dominance, exploitation, and ownership from the time of European colonization and slavery in the United States generally results in white people further resenting Women of Color who cry, especially when they are being raped or their children were taken away, as they have been since the enslavement period. Anita continues,

> With white men, the balance of power Women of Color experience is so uneven, regardless of how we present, that tears are the last thing we want to shed when navigating sexism. The power dynamics of gender are so skewed in favor of white men in the white world and coupled with the underlying racism that is alive every day everywhere for Women of Color; tears only serve to dehumanize us more in the eyes of white men when navigating sexism, making it easier for them to consider us fair game.

In turn, many Women of Color have learned to hide their pain and vulnerability from white people rather than, as Dr. Caprice Hollins shared in a conversation, "risk seeing once again how truly little you care."[2]

White women are also socialized not to see People of Color as capable of experiences or feelings that warrant caring from anyone. We may minimize their concerns in order to avoid our own implication, wondering, "Why are *you* crying?" instead of admitting we don't have the desire to care. When People of Color cry about racism, it makes white women feel bad, as we take it as a personal affront to our own virtue.

While our first response to tears can be to assume we need to comfort, if we do offer support, it is often in a way that exacerbates pain for the Person of Color, while making us feel better. We may propose a solution to the perceived problem in the form of unwarranted advice that calls into question the Person of Color's emotional response, "Maybe if you thought about it this way instead. Maybe if you weren't always seeing racism in the world, you wouldn't experience it so much."

Or we offer a hug. In one workplace conversation about racism that we witnessed, a Woman of Color started crying as she talked about her daily frustrations with racist microaggressions. A white man walked toward her and said, "Can I give you a hug?" Now, she was in no place to refuse. If she didn't hug him, she would be seen as being rude to someone who "just wants to show he cares."

In another multiracial group, a Woman of Color shared a painful story of racism with a white woman. Tilman felt so uncomfortable with the Woman of Color's tears that, despite not knowing her well, she bombarded her with tissues and rubbed the woman's back without invitation. Instead of honoring the Woman of Color's words and message as she took the risk to share, Tilman invaded her space and exacerbated her pain. The Woman of Color had to stop what she was sharing to ask Tilman to STOP touching her, which immediately took the focus off of the important point the Woman of Color was making and toward the reaction of a white woman.

It may then be easier for People of Color to not risk sharing their woundedness around racism when, in those moments
where they are re-experiencing trauma, they then are expected to
address or take care of white people's comfort.

White Women's Tears As a Response to Sexism

White men can act out their anger and are often rewarded for yelling or slamming their fists on the table to make a point. Talk radio
hosts offer several great examples of this. White men are seen as
powerful leaders for the same behaviors that would get anyone
else fired. In conversations about racism, they act out their white
fragility by shutting down or walking out. Some will interrupt or
talk over people and expect every question they have to be discussed by the larger group. We've had white men in workshops
say, "Fine, I just won't say anything anymore," when asked to be
conscious of their airtime.

We've seen white men slam their fists down in meetings, yell
at people they supervise, tower over and lecture people who dis-
agreed with their anti-racist analysis, storm out of the room, and
talk about grabbing women by the pussy with little to no negative
consequences. In fact, many people see these bullying and abusive traits as strong leadership qualities.

When we asked one white man what was going on for him
when he was sighing and crossing his arms, he yelled, "Nothing is
going on for me. You can't make assumptions based on someone's
body language!" Hmm. Guess we were right to think something
was going on.

Many have left the room after saying nothing, only to talk with
other white men about what a waste of time it is to talk about race
in the workplace and question the expertise of the People of Color
leading these sessions.

Historically and currently, white women's liberation on a systemic level depends on white men. For example, we got the right
to vote in the United States because white men made a politically
savvy decision to grant this to us. Given this power imbalance
that persists today, most white women will not risk angering white

men when we want to get our way or are in harm's way. Instead, when we feel frustrated or scared, one strategy that white women have learned is that tears may be a valid and effective way to protect us from, and sometimes work around, sexism.

The typical response to our tears is to comfort and care for us. With white men, this then puts us in the subservient role they expect and are comfortable with. They get to see themselves as our protectors, the white knights who gallop in to rescue us from perceived forms of danger.

Our socialization to be the damsel in distress often results in white women identifying as criers, as Ilsa shares from her experiences.

> I am a crier. If someone in a conversation starts crying, my empathic tears flow, even if I have never met them before. When I was young, my parents dubbed my favorite TV show *Little Tears on the Prairie*. I bawled my way through many movies, from *Malcolm X* to *Up*. I cry when I unintentionally hurt someone, make mistakes, fail tests, learn about unexpected debt I've accrued, when I'm really happy, and when I just need a good cry. Crying is my go-to way of expressing my emotions. And for most of my life, I assumed this was how I was as an individual, based on how my parents raised me, and unrelated to race or gender.

Crying can also help to stop violence and literally save our lives. Tilman's story of childhood abuse illustrates this.

> I grew up learning that tears were meant for home only, and even then, I had to be seriously hurt or upset. According to my family culture, it was not appropriate to cry in public, no matter how difficult the situation. Tears were a sign of weakness and lack of discipline. We were expected to respond to pain, sadness, and fear in calm, rational ways to demonstrate our upper-class superiority and control. We were allowed tears during moments when moved by joy or humor, but not by sadness or pain. This value was deeply ingrained in me.

The rule was relaxed very little at home, where I regularly experienced dysfunction and violence. This is where I learned to use my tears deliberately to buy myself time in moments of extreme pain and fear. If I yelled or screamed, the abuse wouldn't stop. If I cried, because of my family's expectation of toughness and stoicism, my abuser would worry that I was genuinely hurt and often stop long enough for me to get away.

These childhood experiences were what propelled me to explore the sexism connection to white women's tears. I knew that this strategy saved me from more severe danger and harm. I knew that my tears bought me time to think of an escape, and, therefore, I came to deeply appreciate the power of tears when used in this way. This use of tears is an example of the patriarchal bargain many women have to make to survive. I counted on my abuser's sexism to effectively stop him from causing irreparable damage to my body. Where yelling and fighting fueled his fury, crying often managed to stop him because it reminded him of my relative smallness and weakness and his supposed role as protector.

When experiencing sexism, tears call attention to white women's needs, which, as Tilman's story illustrates, can be invaluable to our survival. Whether intentional or not, we can cry and often elicit a sympathetic response where men then listen more closely to what we're saying.

Ilsa shares a story of a time when she recognized in the moment how crying worked to her advantage. Crying wasn't an intentional decision, the tears just "came out of nowhere" (in other words, her forty-some years of sexist and racist socialization).

I was walking home one New Year's Eve with my boyfriend. He was insisting we could walk up a steep hill, and he wanted to take the side streets to avoid drunk pedestrians. I wanted to walk up the main drag to look for a cab or catch a bus. I felt worn out and was not interested in climbing a hill. However, I didn't feel safe just walking away from him and taking my own route by myself. As our argument escalated and I felt he wasn't hearing how tired I was, I began crying. He quickly stopped talking and listened carefully as I expressed my exhaustion through tears. I immediately felt the power shift in the conversation to one where I now had more equal footing and say in the decision of how we got home.

Ilsa realized she could utilize being seen as needing care in order to get her way in the argument. As she felt the power shift, she then made the decision to trade off collusion with sexism for the short-term gain of a comfortable ride home.

While crying can work to our advantage with white men, simultaneously, tears can be seen as a sign of weakness, particularly in male-dominated workspaces. Women who identify as criers may silence themselves if they anticipate their voice breaking when they try to speak. Women quickly apologize for showing any emotion, knowing this might indicate they aren't strong enough to do their jobs. In order to climb the work ladder, women generally need to suppress emotions. As an Asian American woman recently told us her white female boss had a rule that the one thing her employees, most of whom were young women, were not allowed to do at work was cry. Not under any circumstances. The "no-cry" rule of Tilman's family was connected to preparing her for the white male work world, where it was understood that crying was a sign of weakness and lack of control.

Tears for Fears

Although crying can potentially save white women from abuse or help us get heard by white men, the use of tears is a cognitive maladaptation when engaging with People of Color in conversations about racism. A lifetime of socialization has taught many of us to be fearful of Black and Brown people, and our stereotypes of them emerge as we talk about race. Our brain shortcut or "mind-bug" triggers unconscious fear. While it may feel the same physiologically, this fear is not for our actual safety but rather about not wanting to confront the reality of our racism. Our tears are a self-protection against the shame and dissonance we feel about our racist feelings that actively contradict the fallacy of our innate goodness and purity. At the same time, our internalized superiority comes up as we expect ourselves to know more (about everything) than People of Color and worry what might happen if we don't control the direction of the conversation. It is in those moments where we frequently see white women say they feel attacked, then start to choke up. This is unrelated to our actual safety but rather a way to re-center our sense of comfort and control.

In their article, "Getting slammed: white depictions of race discussions as arenas of violence," Robin DiAngelo and Özlem Sensoy analyze discourse in a small group discussion about race that illustrates how the language of violence is used by white women in describing conversations with People of Color. They look at one white woman's response to being challenged around her privilege.

> She claims that if she does not defend herself against these challenges, the only possible outcome is to submit to further abuse via serving as a "punching bag."...By employing terms that connote physical abuse, Amanda taps into the classic discourse that People of Color are inherently dangerous and violent toward whites...Thus, the history of extensive, brutal, and explicit physical violence perpetrated by whites against People of Color—slavery, lynching, whipping, genocide, internment, forced sterilization, and medical experimentation to mention a few—as well as its ideological rationalizations, are trivialized through white claims of a lack of safety when in the rare situation of merely talking about race with People of Color. By claiming victimization, whites obscure the power and privilege we wield and have wielded for centuries.[3]

Because we've been taught to fear People of Color, which upholds white male supremacy, we may erroneously confuse conversations about our privilege as arenas of violence. After stating we are "being drilled," white women often then begin crying. Here we are using the same tools we've developed in dealing with white men to reassert our power, all the while claiming innocence.

This belief about our goodness and the "threat" that recognizing our collusion with racism poses to our sense of goodness is so deeply ingrained in white women that the tears often seem to well up with no conscious thought. We play into the myth of white female innocence. We may even claim the Person of Color, "made me cry," instead of recognizing how we are asserting white supremacy through an act that seemingly makes us appear victimized.

The Impact of White Women's Tears

This contradiction of appearing powerless in order to reclaim power makes it all the more difficult for People of Color to challenge white women who cry. People of Color are now seen as responsible for hurting someone's feelings. They have the choice to apologize to the white woman or appear uncaring and possibly risk losing their jobs.

We are not asserting there is always something intentionally manipulative in white women's tears, although this may well be the case. However, we do need to examine how crying centers whiteness in cross-cultural interactions despite our intentions.

Many Women of Color have talked and written about the impact of white women crying during conversations about racism. In the article, "4 Ways White People Can Process Their Emotions Without Bringing the White Tears," Jennifer Loubriel sums up many of the issues when she writes,

> Oftentimes, in other spaces, your emotions, and the emotions of other white people, are constantly centered, nurtured, and coddled when it comes to conversations about race. Rather than focusing on the lived experiences and

traumas of People of Color when talking about racism, the focus is placed on the host of emotions that white people go through when confronted with racism. Rather than focusing on how People of Color feel on an everyday basis from having to deal with racist institutions, interpersonal relationships, and ideologies, the focus goes to white people just beginning to confront how they benefit from racism on many levels.[4]

White people and People of Color have been socialized to take care of white women. In part, this comes from a sexist and racist belief system that teaches us to see white women as virtuous, weak, and needing protection. In her paper "When White Women Cry: How White Women's Tears Oppress Women of Color," Accapadi notes "The problem for white women is that their privilege is based on accepting the image of goodness, which is powerlessness." This is the particular position of the buffer: we literally access our white privilege through colluding with patriarchal versions of who we are.

It complicates matters when a white woman begins crying and a Person of Color chooses to comfort her. Accapadi captures this dynamic as well by citing Richard Dyer, who explains, "White people set standards of humanity by which they are bound to succeed." A common outcome when there is a conflict is that white societal norms are used to manage the tensions, thus protecting the white woman and problematizing the Person of Color, who is seen as the cause of her tears. So, comforting us is a conscious survival strategy that People of Color have had to learn to the point that it may become innate and reflexive.[5]

Sometimes a Person of Color will immediately apologize for their comment that resulted in a white woman's tears, even when they were making a perfectly legitimate point. Aware of white women's tendency to cry, when they give us feedback People of Color will often plan carefully not only what they want to say but also the tone they will use in order to appear caring or nonthreatening. Other People of Color may shut down in the conversation, as they witness this pattern of centering care for white women far too often. However, if they voice their frustrations, they are likely to be seen as heartless or mean.

Ilana shared an example of this from her experience in multiracial feminist settings, "I'm thinking about, like, me crying and having emotions, and the temptation in the room is to hold the feelings and nurture…Then a couple of Women of Color in the group leave angry because we started talking about racism and we ended coddling the emotions of a white woman."

Our tears may be a response to having our racism directly pointed out. Because we equate feedback around our racist attitudes, assumptions, and actions, with us being essentially bad people, we respond emotionally. My image of myself doesn't match how someone sees me. The more I try to prove I'm not a bad person by showing how sensitive I am and crying, the more I actually confirm my lack of understanding of the dynamics of racism.

Sometimes we cry because we're feeling empathy and connecting with a painful experience a Person of Color is sharing. Other times we're just coming to understand the extent of racism in the world and feel overwhelmed with sadness.

Regardless of the intention or reason behind the tears, when white women's emotions become the central focus of the conversation, this reinforces racism and has a harmful impact on People of Color. There is even a saying, "When white women cry, Black men die." As Dr. Eddie Moore, Jr. points out in his workshops based on his book *The Guide for White Women Who Teach Black Boys*, there is a clear history of white women deliberately lying about Black men and crying to get out of trouble with white men. To illustrate this, Dr. Moore shares a scene from *Rosewood*, a movie that depicts the true story of the brutal massacre in a predominantly African American Florida town in 1923 after a white woman lies about a Black man beating her. Knowing that racial tensions were building in the town, the white woman makes a deliberate scene, screaming and crying that a Black man broke into her house and beat her (but makes sure to insist that he did not rape her). One woman's tears catalyzed a homicidal anger and need to dominate that included the lynching and murder of Black men, women, and children, and burning down of the town with no justice or restitution until 1994.[6]

One way of understanding white women's tears is to see how this same behavior might look in different phases as we move from Immersion to Integration in our identity development model. As you read, we encourage white women to think of a time, or times, when you cried in a conversation about racism. What led you to tears? What were you feeling? Why were you crying? No, really, why were you crying?

Tears in Immersion

Because of our enculturation in white male norms, white women in Immersion may hate it when women cry. We associate tears with weakness and learn to "suck it up." Our parents may punish us for crying by saying, "I'll give you something to cry about." These lessons live in the way we despise ourselves and other women who cry. We laugh and make fun of the woman on *The Bachelor* whose mascara runs down her face. The creators of our media know and exploit this form of internalized sexism.

Having no systemic analysis, white women in the Immersion phase cry because we insist on seeing ourselves as the victims of individuals who don't like us. We take it as a personal affront to seeing ourselves as good, moral people when someone points out our racist attitudes. Celebrity chef Paula Deen offered an example of this stage in her response to accusations of racism and her use of the n-word. While crying, she stated, "I feel like 'embattled' or 'disgraced' will always follow my name. It's like that Black football player who recently came out. He said, 'I just want to be known as a football player. I don't want to be known as a gay football player.' I know exactly what he's saying."[7]

She intentionally compared her experience of being called racist with the discrimination Michael Sam, a Black gay football player, had gone through (notably without remembering his name). Deen used his genuine suffering as a vehicle to rationalize how she felt being called out on her racism. Drawing a false equivalency between institutionalized oppression and personal accountability for racist actions is a common pattern among white people in Immersion. This is similar to white women who voted for Trump, then cried and claimed their views were being misunderstood when People of Color voiced concern with racism in the policies of the administration.

Tilman remembers a time when she was young teenager and frequently went to a blatantly white supremacist country club that did not allow People of Color or Jewish people to become members. *The Washington Post* wrote an article that called out this racism, and Tilman's father was mentioned on page one. When another child who also frequently went to this club ironically called out Tilman's father as racist and embarrassed her in front of friends, Tilman burst into tears and proclaimed, "You just don't understand how difficult it is for my father!" These tears halted any critical discussion of the racism they all benefited from and ricocheted the concern away from the point about racism and back to Tilman and her hurt feelings. The person who originally called Tilman's father out was chastised and made to feel disrespectful and audacious for even bringing the topic up.

As illustrated in the story of the staff training at the beginning of this chapter, the resulting conversation typically re-centers the white woman's experience. Those who name the behavior are seen as cruel. People jump in to defend the white woman's individual character, reassuring us that we are, through her, good people, rather than looking at the way our behaviors uphold systems of oppression.

Tears in Capitulation

With growing awareness of sexism in the Capitulation stage, white women may insist on safe spaces for race conversations. They confuse safety with comfort, essentially asserting, "I want to be able to say whatever I want to say and not be challenged in a way that makes me uncomfortable." Which usually means not being challenged at all.

In a 2014 episode of *The Daily Show*, four fans of the Washington, DC, football team were invited to talk about why they supported the mascot. At the same time, four Native Americans, members of the group *The 1491s*, who had worked to change the mascot, spoke in a separate room about why they thought it was harmful. Afterward, the Native Americans came into the room with the fans and began asking them questions.

Kelli O'Dell, a white woman who was previously employed by the Washington football team, and whose internet presence was devoted to her support of the team and mascot, began crying. Knowing she was about to get in trouble and possibly face repercussions for her racist actions, Kelli pivoted. She said she felt threatened and later tried to file a police report. She told *The Washington Post* afterward, "The Native Americans accused me of things that were so wrong. I felt in danger. I didn't consent to that. I'm going to be defamed."[8]

It is common in the Capitulation stage for a white woman to cry in the moment, then later seek retribution. We may also say we're going to have to "agree to disagree" if we start to feel emotional in the conversation. This then asserts our power in stopping an uncomfortable moment before we have to examine our racist assumptions.

Tilman provides another example of this pattern from when she worked at a small teacher education college, where she often co-taught a class on the social and political contexts of the education system. Tilman was proud of the fact that as a white woman she was an integral member of this teaching team, especially during the years when classes were offered in a Spanish/English dual language format. Though she didn't speak Spanish, Tilman felt she was grounded in course content and with dual-language strategies, and this led her to feel a sense of importance in her role on this team.

During one of the class cohorts, it became clear that one of the bilingual faculty members of Color didn't want to interpret for the English-speaking students. Even though this woman was a full-time faculty member, had a more advanced degree than Tilman, and held more status at the college, Tilman felt righteous and irritated that her colleague was not supporting English-speaking students who were predominantly white.

One day, during an initially friendly conversation, Tilman took it upon herself to communicate her frustration to the bilingual faculty member. She did this while smiling and cloaking the issue as concern for the students when it was really about her desire to feel comfortable in the class herself. When the faculty member rightfully became furious with her, Tilman acted stunned. While she didn't cry in the moment, she was immediately defensive and hurt that her perspective had created such a visceral and angry response. There was no recognition or self-reflection on Tilman's part that she had been out of line or racist in her approach to the situation, and that she was more concerned with her own needs over those of her colleague's. The conversation was cut short because both women had to go to a campus meeting together.

In the meeting, everyone could tell there was tension between the two women, and while Tilman didn't cry during this meeting, it was obvious that she was upset. At the end of the meeting the tears came. Once the bilingual faculty member was gone, Tilman covertly sought out a small group of people with whom she not only cried but made a point to blame the woman for being insensitive, unreceptive to feedback, and unresponsive to the students' needs. Her tears were well-timed and manipulative, and they paved a way for her to appear less racist while also re-centering her ideas of how things should be done. The ultimate result was that Tilman reasserted her primacy in this situation. The fact that it also ended a collegial relationship between Tilman and the faculty member was the price Tilman paid for her need for control and comfort.

By crying in a smaller group, white women may gather support behind the Person of Color's back. This can cause more insidious harm to the people who confronted them, with no chance for the Person of Color to respond or hold them responsible. This is evident most often in Capitulation, where we appear to cave in at the time and then use our weaponized tears as the proverbial knife in the back.

Tears in Defense

In Defense, white women are conscious of institutionalized sexism and some of the dynamics of racism. However, we still lack awareness of how our whiteness has influenced our identity. When we cry in the Defense stage, it is usually to prove to the people around us how much we understand racism and how much they are not understanding just how much we understand racism.

When Ilsa was in college, she went to an environmental justice conference with a multiracial group of about twelve students. At some point, People of Color decided they all wanted to stay together at one of the host's houses, which left the white people all rooming together in another house. Ilsa felt frustrated because she wanted to be included with the People of Color. Throughout that weekend, she experienced what she deemed to be exclusion and mistreatment, particularly from one Black woman. At one point, Ilsa started crying and told other people she didn't feel she was being treated fairly by this woman. The Black woman apologized to Ilsa, while others in the group reassured her that they liked her and Ilsa was wanted.

This was exactly what Ilsa expected when she cried and how she felt she deserved to be treated. However, they never talked about why the People of Color might want to all room together when traveling to a predominantly white city out of town, or what was problematic in Ilsa's assumption this had anything to do with her personally. By centering her feelings of being excluded, Ilsa not only missed an opportunity to learn more about experiences different from her own, she also interrupted the potential for People of Color to have a chance to do work that did not involve her.

Another example of Defense comes from a workshop Ilsa was co-facilitating with a Woman of Color a few years ago. They informed the group we'd be breaking into race-based caucuses after spending a day and a half working together. Upon hearing this, a white woman began crying and told the group she didn't see how this would be beneficial, especially since the person she'd learned the most from and cared the most about, her boyfriend, was Latino and would be in the other group. We told her to share her concerns in the caucus where we would talk further. When we took a break to split into the two groups, she continued crying and he immediately went over to comfort and reassure her.

During the white caucus, we spent some time talking about her concerns, but not much. Many other people were upset with breaking into separate groups and felt sorry for her, saying we shouldn't have cut her off and should have given her more time to air her concerns in the large group. All told, this took about fifteen minutes of the hour we had.

At the same time, the People of Color caucus spent the entire time talking about the impact of white women's tears on the group. They discussed the role People of Color play in comforting white women as well as frustration with having her emotions then become the topic of their entire conversation. When we came back together, many from the People of Color caucus were angry the white group had not spent more time discussing this as well.

Multiple characteristics of Defense showed up here. The assumption that white people are entitled to learn from People of Color about racism and the expectation that everyone take care of a white woman crying were clear. As a facilitator, Ilsa's failure to see how much that moment impacted the room and spend more time on it in the caucus essentially minimized the concerns of People of Color. Due to her discomfort and uncertainty, Ilsa moved away from the key moment of conflict into a discussion and an agenda that gave her a greater sense of security. This often happens with white people in management positions, where they avoid racial conflict and center their comfort in staff meetings. Sticking to the agenda is a powerful tool of white supremacy culture that intentionally centers whiteness.

White women with an understanding of our white privilege will also resort back to Defense and our marginalized identity as women when we feel a challenge to our power. In a meeting a few years ago, Women of Color were talking candidly about how they did not like white women. A white woman began crying while she angrily explained to them how unjust it was that they would target white women and completely ignore the problematic behaviors of white men in the room. Due to internalized sexism, this is a common pattern—white men get a pass while white women are villainized. However, the way this woman pointed it out signified how she took their general comments personally and then took up a great deal of airtime in lecturing them from a position of superiority. Her crying made it more difficult for others to challenge her back without it being assumed they would somehow harm her.

Tears when Transitioning to Projection

The transition from Defense to Projection often happens through a deep, emotional experience. For white women, these are times when we feel the pain of first accepting the extent of racism and the fact that we have unconsciously thought and acted in ways that cause harm to People of Color. This happens largely because we grow up in a society that deliberately keeps us sheltered from the truth of our racist history and then tells us to disbelieve People of Color who attempt to share a different narrative. These are periods of profound guilt about institutional oppression and shame around our collusion.

Beth Yohe reflected on one of those moments.

One of the times when I was most problematic was when I was in college, eighteen years ago or so. We were on a civil rights tour. I went to a university in the South, and I was the only white student on the trip. So, it was myself, and I can't remember how many people, less than twenty, but [all the others were] People of Color.

And I was definitely in that place of resistance in a weird sort of way. Like, I was ready to accept that racism exists and that I had privilege sort of, but I don't remember if at that time it was the language I would have used. But you know, you are looking at that history and all I saw was other white people who did horrible things. I was in this place of, like, really struggling with that...

But the way it showed up was I took up so much space on that trip, right? I was crying, and all those other students were supportive, loving people who took care of the one white girl who was falling apart, right? I don't remember now how I felt about it, but you know after I went through training and when I started to think back...It was a very pivotal part in my life, and I can see it that way now. But now I can also look back and oh...I was such a white woman...

I was working through that identity of having to accept that I was white and that meant that I was connected to these people, and so I think it was that. I think it was wanting to prove that I was a different kind of white person. I think it was all happening at once, and it came out in tears because it was something as a white woman I was allowed to do and express in that way...It was a chunk to work through; the acceptance of my role in racism...

And then I got to a place in different parts of my life where white women cry and People of Color care-take. I get so annoyed...I'd just be so mad at the white women and just be like, stop crying, you know, just get over yourself. It took me a long time to connect those two things in a significant way.

Similar to Beth, when Ilsa was in college, she first learned she had white privilege. After watching the movie *The Color of Fear* with a multicultural group of people who all worked together in the campus Women's Center, she began sobbing. In the moment, it was a raw, emotional response. Reflecting back, she believes these tears came from the shame she felt in being white and the many ways she and people who looked like her had hurt People of Color. Ilsa felt deeply connected to the harm caused by her people.

At the same time, her emotional response then became the focal point of the conversation, as she expected it would be. Ilsa would have been rocked further to her core had the group not paid attention to her pain, failing to see how other stories were then lost as she was comforted. She doesn't remember anyone else's response to the movie.

There was also something about the depth of her emotion that set her apart from other white people. As Beth said, she wanted them to see her as a different kind of white person. Someone who felt this bad about racism could not be racist. These moments can propel white women into the Projection phase. It is a combination of learning about racism while deeply feeling the impact. If we stay in an intellectual understanding only, we often will not grow in the same way. This is where white caucus experiences can be particularly valuable, as our growth then doesn't happen at the expense of People of Color's pain in shepherding us through our emotions while learning.

Tears in Projection

White women's anger about our previous ignorance of racism shows up in full force in Projection. This may be directed internally and felt as shame or externally in blaming other white people.

Because our understanding of white privilege is new, we rely on a set of rules for the "right" behavior. Through workshops, articles, books like this one, or conversations with Women of Color, many of us learn that our tears can be problematic. We interpret this as the rule, "Thou shalt not cry!" If another white woman cries, as Beth illustrated, we become frustrated with her and may be the first to point out how damaging she is to the group. This will not be a statement made to support her understanding and growth; it is a personal attack on another white woman who we want to distance ourselves from.

Learning about racism gives us feelings, but we believe we shouldn't cry. We are more likely to hide emotions in Projection, crying to ourselves or icing over our tears with some of the same messages we've got from our sexist socialization. "I should suck it up, stop being so sensitive, so needy, stop being such an idiot." Essentially, our internalized sexism tells us we're worthless because we're racist and our whiteness won't let us see how we can still be good people and do racist things.

This then gives us limited options for responding when we start to cry involuntarily in a discussion about racism. We have seen white women in what we recognize as the Projection phase run out of the room in the middle of a courageous conversation because they had started crying and said they "didn't want to impact the group." Ironically, someone running out of the room does tend to still impact the group.

Another white woman choked back tears as she was processing the loss of her grandmother while a multiracial group wrote poems about their childhood experiences. However, she said she didn't want to cry about this because she believed her tears would negatively impact the People of Color in the room. This overgeneralization of new rules, common in human development, can leave us seeming cold and disconnected. We may be unwilling to share stories of our own painful experiences in cross-cultural settings, thus inadvertently thwarting authentic relationships with People of Color.

Tilman shared a similar moment when she was participating in an invitational institute with a multiracial group of anti-racism educators and activists. This was a community of people Tilman deeply admired and felt honored to be connected to. The focus of the institute was trauma, and each person shared deep and painful experiences from their lives. Almost all of the participants cried while they talked and while they listened. When it became Tilman's turn to share, she recounted a painful story about childhood abuse, and when she felt she was about to cry, she stopped to proclaim that she knew it wasn't okay to cry in a multiracial setting, so she'd stop there.

After the discussion, one of the facilitators, a Woman of Color, asked to talk to Tilman. She explained to her that, while white women's tears were usually problematic for People of Color, in this particular circumstance, her tears were welcomed because of the context of trauma and connection of the participants. Before she could finish her sentence, Tilman cut in, saying she could not be one of "those" white women who took up space with her tears. The Woman of Color very patiently stopped Tilman and asked her to listen and believe her as she explained that the context in which a white woman cries is important to consider and that there were no hard and fast rules to be followed. At that point, the Woman of Color hugged Tilman and walked away.

One of the ways whiteness shows up in all stages is our tendency to intellectualize and use heady analysis of racism without connecting this to our hearts. W. E. B. Du Bois wrote about the psychological toll racism takes on white people. In the chapter "Of Soul and White Folks" in Mab Segrest's *Born to Belonging*, she builds on his work, writing about the cognitive dissonance involved in having to see ourselves as separate from People of Color to perpetuate atrocities against them, including enslavement of African Americans. She writes, "Necessary to the slave system was the masters' blocked sensation of its pain, an aesthetic that left him insensible not only to the fellow human beings he enslaved but to the testimony of his senses that might have contradicted ideologies of slavery." The pattern of intellectual justifications, such as doctors asserting that Black people don't feel pain in the same way, had a dehumanizing impact on whites as well.

Instead of crying, white women in Projection lean toward hyper-intellectualizing. Stuffing down our tears then reinforces the same harmful pattern of becoming emotionally distant from People of Color. Segrest refers to this as "the soul-destroying anesthesia necessary to the maintenance of power."[9]

Having read this, a person in Projection might then ask, "So what should I do? First, you tell me not to cry, now you're telling me I should cry?" Yes, both.

Tears in Balance

White women in Balance recognize that our tears impact People of Color, regardless of why we may be crying. We understand the importance of context and relationship in different situations. For example, crying when relating to a shared experience of losing a family member is very different from crying when confronted with one's own racist beliefs. We then make deliberate decisions around how we will handle our emotions, or, if overcome with tears, what we will do in that particular situation.

In Balance, white women who know we cry often will carry tissues with us. When we do begin crying in a conversation about racism, we will continue in the conversation without centering our emotional response, become curious about a Person of Color's perspective, and stay engaged by speaking through our tears rather than shutting down. We remember that we can cry, think, and listen at the same time and that one action does not preclude the other from happening. If appropriate, we may take a brief moment to explain why we are having the emotional response without faulting someone else.

Ways this may sound include the following:

- "I'm crying because it is hard for me to hear my actions had that impact. I'd like to hear more if you're willing to share, so I can make sure my actions and core values are better aligned in the future."
- "I'm sorry for the impact my crying might be having on others in the room. I don't want my tears to become the focus of this conversation."
- "I'm crying because I'm connecting to what you're saying."
- "I care a great deal about justice in the world. Right now, I think I'm crying because I feel how profoundly racism damages us."
- "I'm not sure why I'm becoming emotional. I'm okay and will share as I can."
- "I appreciate you checking in. I brought my tissues because I know I tend to cry. I don't need anything else right now."

Other ways white women can better navigate our tears is to talk unflinchingly about racism, learn the reality of our history from books and articles by People of Color so we are not so surprised by their stories, and do our own processing with other white people. This may be in a formal white caucus in the workplace or community (such as a local chapter of Showing Up for Racial

Justice) or in a book group and conversations with friends. These actions will help us stay in the stage of Balance.

White caucuses are a racial justice tool designed for white people to grapple with white privilege and our anti-racist identity together. Crying in a white caucus doesn't have the same impact as in a multiracial space. White-only groups are a great place to explore what lies beneath white women's tears.

Ilana's story below illustrates an awareness of herself, knowledge of white privilege, and the skills to better navigate her emotions that came from these spaces.

> Now, working more within caucus work, it's about redirecting where those emotions show up. When is it appropriate for those emotions to show up?
>
> And also, there's a resiliency piece that I've learned. I've only learned it through experiencing significant loss. I lost my brother last year. It's the hardest thing I've ever survived…I'm a stronger person now because of it. Like, I don't cry about racism like I did before…
>
> And the way I believe this relates to whiteness and white supremacy and racism is that my guess is that Folks of Color have experienced more loss and pain and suffering earlier and, therefore, had to survive that and build resiliency around that. To where showing up at a conversation about racism, they're not going to sit and cry, even though like the pain to folks of color is really fucking significant…
>
> That's why I think of the phenomenon of white women crying, or whiteness taking up space with emotions, is a phenomenon that we haven't had to be challenged with or experience loss collectively. And, therefore, when we come in these spaces we're just like, "Oh my god, my comfort zone has been interrupted." I've only really been able to get that through the loss of my brother.

We also have not had to confront the realities of racism, so it is not only our comfort zone being interrupted but our whole concept of ourselves as morally good.

Only through doing our work around how we've been hurt and hurt others as a result of oppression can those of us who are criers hope to show up as allies. White women benefit from reflecting more deeply on the intersection of sexism and white privilege to work through our pain that can result in inappropriately placed emotions.

In Balance, white women may feel a disconnect between how they are choosing to show up and their internal turmoil. As the name implies, we are carefully putting one foot in front of the other like a gymnast on a beam, attempting to reconcile head and heart. When we wipe away our tears with a tissue, we intellectually know that a Person of Color's experience or even criticism is not *only* about the racist harm we caused. At the same time, we may feel all kinds of internal quaking. In other words, we know the feedback is not all about us, but it still feels like it is an affront to our deeply socialized sense of ourselves as nice people. We have to intentionally choose to see their story, learn more of the historical context of their experience, and reflect on our contribution to their pain.

Tears in Integration

White women shift in Integration to a steadier walk, resulting in better alignment of our core values with our external actions. We have addressed many of the underlying issues and experiences of oppression that might have brought up tears in earlier stages. We've gained a deep knowledge of structural racism. A white woman is unlikely to feel triggered and respond emotionally to accusations of racism, for example, because she is not working to prove her own non-racist identity. Rather, she recognizes she was socialized in racist systems and is continually striving to undo racism. She simultaneously holds the integrated reality of her actions with collective racialized and gendered experiences.

When we do cry out of a genuine, empathic connection with a Person of Color or because of our personal pain, we've internalized ways of responding to the complex racial dynamics so as not to center whiteness through our tears. As stated earlier, even white women crying in the stage of Integration can negatively impact a person or group. It is how we respond openly and seek a deeper connection that changes.

Because we have years of sexist and racist socialization, we have to over-practice until this becomes how we are in the world. As Dr. Caprice D. Hollins says in workshops, "We have to over-practice new ways of being." This happens through intentional, concerted effort, many years of cross-cultural engagement, anti-racist activism, and, if we can afford it, some serious therapy.

These moments are fleeting. We might be in Integration for five minutes, then find ourselves back to using our Defense tool-kit. We believe this is a way of being to continually strive for, not a place many white women operate from daily.

Beyond Tears

There are a number of behaviors that might show up in multiple stages in different ways. Applying a race and gender lens to our behaviors means shifting from seeing ourselves solely as individuals and recognizing how these social and political constructs influence our actions and outcomes for groups of people.

Just as we've said "I'm a crier," white women can try finishing the sentences "I'm someone who…," "I'm a…" Are we agenda driven? Data oriented? Introverted? Controlling? Perfectionists? Try analyzing how internalized sexism and white privilege contributed to that identity and think about how it might look different in each of the six stages.

11

If What, Now What?

When we view living in the european mode only as a problem
to be solved, we rely solely upon our ideas to make us free,
for these were what the white fathers told us were precious.

But as we come more in touch with our own ancient, non-
european consciousness of living as a situation to be experienced
and interacted with, we learn more and more to cherish our
feelings, and to respect those hidden sources of our power from
where true knowledge and, therefore, lasting action comes.

— Audre Lorde

IF WHILE READING the book so far you've been wondering, "But what do I do about this?" you're in good company. Many of us recognize the problem, and we want an answer. We tell ourselves we would have changed institutional racism a long time ago if we just had the formula that worked, the data on successful programs that have closed the opportunity gap in other schools, the recruiting strategy to bring more People of Color into our organizations, the checklist of anti-racist behaviors.

Much of this information has been available to us for many years. So, why haven't we changed?

Systems of institutionalized heteropatriarchy and white supremacy are complex and resilient to any quick fix. And human beings bring vast differences to any interaction. The deep work needed to reach Balance and Integration may happen along any number of paths but will happen only through our sustained effort in countering daily messages intended to keep us in Immersion. We have to collectively and creatively support one another on this journey toward personal and institutional change.

We started this book with the story of how we came together with MG to create a practice of supportive, non-competitive, and critical reflection and action around our internalized sexism and white superiority. With each gathering of our small group, focus groups, caucuses, and workshops, we have expanded this practice together. At the end of our workshops, we've asked the women to brainstorm strategies for continuing to move toward Integration. The following list was generated from all of these groups. We encourage you to add to it.

Grow Awareness and Knowledge

Commit to an on-going process.

Given our socialization into complex systems of privilege and oppression, we could spend a lifetime uncovering the ways we've internalized superiority and inferiority around multiple dimensions of identity. In the time it has taken us to write this book, we've noticed many ways our previously unconscious stereotypes showed up. Sometimes we uncover our biases through reading an article or book, listening to a podcast, attending a conference, or having a rich conversation. Sometimes it happens through our stumbling and bumbling. We must not only recognize our growth as an on-going process but also have the internal motivation to seek out new information and try out new, often messy practices.

Know who you are as an ethnic and cultural being.

One of the manifestations of white supremacy in the United States is the mythical melting pot; the assimilation process that considers the Anglo-American middle-class cultural pattern as ideal.[1] As white people are constantly lured toward this ideal with the benefits of white privilege, we simultaneously lose an understanding of our ethnic and cultural identities. This disconnection from our roots can leave us feeling adrift and unsettled for reasons we can't articulate. Understanding our family histories if we have access to them can connect us to our family cultures and cultural values. The way we wake up, go to sleep, eat our meals, raise our children, work, and socialize are all indicators of culture. By understanding our cultural values, we can understand our reasons for much of what we do, instead of assuming everyone does things the same way we do them and pathologizing cultural differences. If we can't name and own our values, it may be difficult for us to imagine why someone else may care so deeply about their values. Without this self-awareness, we will tend to default to the white, middle-class cultural patterns and expect all around us to do the same. This limits our ability to be effective cross-cultural practitioners.

Be reflective about what needs are being met by your behavior.

In their book, *Immunity to Change*, Keagan and Laskow Leahy point out that our current behavior won't change if we don't address the underlying need being met by the way we are acting.[2] For example, a white woman we met in a workshop needed to be liked by People of Color because this reinforced her identity as "not racist" or an ally. When she called out white people on their racist behaviors by name-calling and shaming them on social media, she got a lot of positive feedback from People of Color. This reinforced her behavior, and she was not willing to try a new approach to engaging with other white people until she first interrogated her motivations for trying to shame them.

Avoid dichotomous, either/or thinking.

When we get stuck in binary thinking, it limits our ability to creatively problem solve. For example, someone might ask, "Are you saying I have to respond to ALL microaggressions or I'm a racist?" Instead, let's think of a third or fourth or even fifth option.

This type of mindset also causes us to see people, including ourselves, as good or bad. Since being racist is bad, we may then respond defensively when we make mistakes. Because white women's access to privilege often depends on us being "good and nice," we are particularly susceptible to the good/bad narrative. To move forward, we can either give up letting "goodness" be a primary identity or recognize that good people can also do racist things. Those are two ways to progress, what would be another option?

Be open to the idea that your intent
might not match the impact of your behavior.
It is hard to set aside the myths of our goodness to truly examine how we've unintentionally hurt people and much easier to assume they are being too sensitive. In nearly all groups with meeting agreements, assume good intentions will be listed. Truly assuming good intentions would mean we wouldn't need to talk about intent at all and could focus all of our energy on impact. In reality, this agreement is usually used to dismiss any unintentional harm.

We often use a metaphor of a bicyclist being hit by a car to illustrate this. The driver was the person at fault in the accident. Instead of talking about whether they intended to hit the cyclist or whether they are a good driver, we'll first examine what the person who got hit needs.

Take care of and love yourself.
When we are rested, well-fed, and healthy, we tend to have more ability to be open and flexible. A person who wears herself out through nonstop activism doesn't serve any movement for justice. There will always be something more we could be doing, so each of us needs to recognize our limitations, stretch them sometimes, and give ourselves the space to recoup our energy at other times.

By recognizing the systemic nature of oppression, we can begin to lovingly forgive ourselves for our mistakes, past, present, and future. Internal self-derision may lead to short-term change but will not sustain us for the long journey ahead. This is also likely to lead to deriding those who remind us of mistakes we have made, making it more difficult to extend the empathy necessary to invite them to also change. It's not easy for Ilsa to approach white women with their hair in locks that remind her of her younger self. As RuPaul says, "If you can't love yourself, how the hell you gonna love somebody else?"[3]

Continually grow your knowledge of privilege and power.
We could spend a lifetime learning more about the history and context of white supremacy culture and heteropatriarchy. Even understanding those words might take several months or years. We've been taught lies and half-truths. Growing our knowledge means unlearning, a more difficult process than if our media, government, schools, and families had better educated us in the first place.

Holding ourselves responsible for further developing our analysis means we are continually applying an equity lens to our personal interactions and the organizations where we work, worship, and play. We don't have to fully understand all of the dynamics to take action (that sure creates a useful excuse to not act), and it helps to collectively reflect in an on-going way.

Empathize.
This includes connecting with People of Color by listening and believing their stories. We often hear white allies say, "I will never know what it is like to be a Person of Color." While this statement is true, it does not mean we shouldn't do our darndest to try to understand and, especially, to see how we have been taught not to see People of Color as fully human, and how that has dehumanized us.

We also need to practice empathy with other white people. Hurt people will lash out to hurt others. Systemic racism and sexism hurt everyone, even as we may be receiving the benefits of white privilege. When we recognize this, it is easier to make empathic connections with other white people who we might otherwise want to dismiss or distance ourselves from. If we as white people cannot talk with other white people about our racist assumptions, whether intentional or not, then there is no way we will be able to change our institutions. If we as white people do not help other white people to see the ways we can work together to address institutional racism, we leave the full weight of that work on the shoulders of People of Color.

Using Awareness and Knowledge to Inform Skills

Pay Attention Now—PAN.

Kathy Obear coined this acronym as a reminder to notice through a race lens what is happening internally and in relation with others.[4] She encourages us to do this without making up a story about what is happening and to reserve judgment or assumption. We might say to another white woman, "I noticed you just walked across the room very quickly and tell this Latina woman, 'I need you to tell me how to connect with your community.'" We reflect back what we see in a neutral tone that invites further discussion.

Through practice in this kind of noticing, we can get better at recognizing race and gender dynamics. This is especially helpful for white people who have not had to pay attention to how our whiteness matters in small ways every day. You may want to keep a journal of what you noticed about whiteness for a week, month, or year to reinforce this practice (try starting with one day).

This can also be used in an organization to name power dynamics as they are happening. When we notice through a lens of race and gender, we're not only paying attention to what is happening but also to who is privileged or marginalized by behaviors and decisions. A simple practice to put in place is to have someone in a meeting take data on who speaks and for how long. We might notice that more white men are speaking and there are Women of Color in the group who we have not heard from. We can recognize when there are no women or People of Color at the table for an important decision. By naming this out loud without assumption, we invite others to address group dynamics. Organizations that value transparency at this level create a more welcoming environment.

We might also notice our white privilege and internalized sexism before we act on it. For example, we realize before we interrupt a Woman of Color who is talking and choose not to insert our viewpoint into the conversation when we've already spoken twice. Actively paying attention is the first step to interrupting learned patterns of behavior that reinforce oppression.

Sometimes just recognizing our behaviors causes us to change. In *Blind Spot: Hidden Biases of Good People*, Benaji and Green-wald point to the research on implicit bias that indicates acknowledging we have bias leads to showing less bias.[5] This is part of the value we see in creating an identity development model where we recognize patterns of behavior, such as competition, then actively choose to do something different.

Stop, Take a Breath—STAB.

When we breathe, more oxygen goes to our brain and we can think more clearly. The science of implicit bias tells us that when we are in a hurry, our stereotypes are more likely to show up because we're operating on autopilot rather than activating our best anti-bias thinking. Many spiritual practices also incorporate noticing the breath. In other words, we can all agree breathing is good.

And yet, in stressful situations, we often hold our breath or rush through making a decision.

Tilman, MG, and Ilsa created the acronym STAB—Stop, Take a Breath (aka our favorite acronym of all time)—to help us remember to pause long enough to breathe. This is especially helpful because it is in those moments when we feel like lashing out that STAB-bing is most useful to redirect our anger. It also makes us laugh at ourselves, which has a calming effect under stress.

Being in the present moment as much as possible, what some refer to as mindfulness, allows for a more genuine connection with one another. When we STAB, we pause long enough to take in what is happening, rather than moving forward down a pre-programmed path of reacting. As one workshop participant put it, "I need to stay close to my breath and body."

Kenneth Jones and Tema Okun identify a *sense of urgency* as one of the components of white supremacist culture, describing it as a "continued sense of urgency that makes it difficult to take time to be inclusive, encourage democratic and/or thoughtful decision-making, to think long-term, to consider consequences."[6]

When we STAB, we can better recognize the perceived time constraints that are causing us to default to white supremacy in our organizational policies.

Try to be curious rather than judgmental and righteous.
When we are triggered by someone or something, remaining curious can be extraordinarily difficult and feel almost impossible— or undesirable. After all, I'm so clearly right and you're so clearly wrong. In these moments, we may imagine we are under attack, so we feel we must attack back. While this can provide temporary gratification, it usually shuts down forward movement and understanding. Curiosity strengthens our capacity for engaging in cross-cultural conversations, interrupting oppressive statements, and increasing self-awareness.

We can ask ourselves,

- "I wonder what I might not understand about this experience because mine is so different."
- "I wonder what this person would have to give up to see how their sexist behavior is hurting others."
- "I wonder where that emotion came from. I reacted much more strongly to that situation than I expected."
- "I'm feeling defensive. I wonder why."

These questions tend to arise when we give ourselves a moment to STAB, and they often lead to creating bridges instead of larger canyons.

Interrupt Oppression

Get ready.
It can be very easy to make up a story about why we didn't speak up when we heard a microaggression. We may tell ourselves there wasn't enough time, the person wouldn't listen anyway, we didn't know the person well enough, it was the wrong place, we didn't know what to say, and on and on. Whether or not these stories are true, they provide a convenient way for us to not interrupt oppression and still feel good about ourselves.

Prepare for how you will bring up the reality of race dynamics in a variety of situations, and recommit yourself each day to living in alignment with your values. This might be done by practicing talking with people who agree with your perspective before entering into a more challenging conversation with someone who does not. Try role-playing different situations. We love the *Theater of the Oppressed* work of Augusto Boal in recognizing the power of acting out a variety of responses to solve problems in communities.[7]

After a difficult interaction at work or a hard conversation, we'll call one another or other social justice co-conspirators to talk about what happened and what we might do differently in the future. This debriefing helps us prepare for the inevitable next time.

Become comfortable with discomfort.

There are more reasons than not for white women to be uncomfortable in these conversations. Some of us may associate passion or anger in conversations with unsafe situations. We may hold ourselves to an unrealistic standard of perfection. Perhaps we worry we won't know what to say, and we feel we should have the "right" words when People of Color trust us with their stories. Many of us have learned to take care of people, and we're uncomfortable any time we perceive someone else to be experiencing pain that we can't fix.

We've also been taught to uphold a social contract that dictates white men should not feel discomfort. When the authors have interrupted white men's sexist and racist behaviors, we've often got a paternalistic reaction from the men, telling us we are out of line or lack enough expertise. We've had to become comfortable with angry reactions, being lectured to, and having white men storm out of the room. We've had other white women become upset with us for the way we treated men. White women justify their male colleagues' behaviors and make us the problem, rather than recognizing that racism and white privilege is the problem.

Whether it is the discomfort of someone else's pain or our own, recognizing this as a natural part of uprooting oppression can help us on the journey to Balance and Integration. We need to be willing to sit in the fire, moving toward rather than away from the flame. This might feel messy and uncertain, a good indicator we are forging a new path.

Use "I" statements.

It feels very different to hear someone tell us we're wrong than to hear someone say they felt upset by our comments. Marshall Rosenberg's work on Nonviolent Communication highlights a process of naming behavior, stating how you feel, and then making a sincere request of the other person.[8] For (a real) example, "When you dressed up like a Japanese schoolgirl on Halloween, I was offended. Even though I know you didn't mean it this way, I see that as making fun of someone else's culture. Can we talk more about the impact of choosing a costume that is based on a race or culture?" This is a simple formula that often involves a much longer conversation.

As the example above illustrates, we don't have to speak up on behalf of someone else. We speak up from our perspective, even though the racist comment or action was directed toward another person or group. This involves understanding the fact that racism hurts all of us and no one is free while some are oppressed.

Using "I" statements situates ourselves in this work too. Instead of making it about "those people over there" who are racist, we see ourselves as learners. Sharing our own mistakes, and the resulting growth, models for others what it looks like to learn and continue, rather than become defensive and shut down.

Telling our stories to one another brings us closer. People may still dismiss our ideas, but when we care about one another it is harder to do something we know hurts or offends them. When someone is reluctant to change their oppressive behavior, we can still draw boundaries. We might tell a relative, "I know you care about me, and you know how much it bothers me when you say that. I don't want you to use that word around me."

A note on nonviolent communication: We have heard People of Color recoil with examples like these and think that Rosenberg is letting white people off the hook—or going out of the way to make us feel "safer." At the same time, many People of Color embrace his work and teach similar examples. This is another illustration of how any strategy is useful only in as far as it brings people into work for justice and serves those most marginalized. It doesn't surprise us that People of Color aren't all in agreement on the best way to do this.

Say what's in your gut.

Our bodies often pick up on oppressive situations before our minds do. There have been a number of times where we sensed something was amiss, didn't speak up, and later felt regret. For example, we noticed a white man dominating a conversation but failed to interrupt him. Even if our gut is wrong, we can still ask a question about what we think we're noticing. The risk in not saying something is far greater than speaking up.

One manifestation of internalized white supremacy and internalized sexism is the idea that we have to articulate everything perfectly and succinctly. An easy silence-breaker is to just ask, "Can we talk about what just happened?" There are times when we haven't known exactly why something is wrong, but we do know that it is. Each time we have spoken in those moments, we have felt relief, even if we didn't get support or the outcome we hoped for.

Be aware of how you compete with other white women to be the best-white-anti-racist-ally.

There is no trophy for projecting the best anti-racist identity. (We know; we were disappointed too when we first learned this.) Most white women we know who have experienced the phase we call Projection can identify a time when they distanced themselves from other white women. One of the key reasons we elected to write this book collaboratively was to strengthen our ability to build authentic and non-competitive relationships with other white women. This is an antidote to the learned and internalized practice of competing with one another, which ultimately divides us and hurts our ability to confront sexism and white privilege.

We've worked in organizations where white women "allies" take great joy in naming every mistake another white person makes and tearing them apart. Usually, People of Color are then left to pick up the pieces of all the broken white people because their livelihood depends on it.

Don't view every incident of sexism/white privilege as a battle.
If we approach people as if we are at war, they will likely also see us as the enemy and respond with an attack. A well-known battle tactic is to dehumanize the other. Seeing someone's humanity first will help us engage a person in a way that invites them into a conversation, even and especially when we might have good reason to be upset with their behavior. One prompt we have found useful is, "You're probably not aware…"

A while back we started hearing the phrase "calling-in" rather than "calling-out." If I'm trying to call you out on your racist actions, you will likely feel my righteous indignation. If I'm trying to call you into a conversation about racism, the goal is to bring you into a movement for change, so we can all benefit from our collective knowledge and experience.

Know when to drop it.
Sometimes letting go in a conversation is better than continuing. For (a real) example, if we find ourselves getting into a debate with someone over whether they should change the name of the Washington, DC, football team when they flew to Seattle for the weekend just to see said team; and if the people we're talking to are becoming more defensive and rooted in their position, and we're becoming more animated the longer we talk; it might be more useful to stop arguing. It is important to remember we can't control how and when people learn (so frustrating!). Know you planted seeds and it may take a different person (another DC

football fan), a different time (not at 11 pm at the bar), or a different approach (buy everyone shots!) to move that person to change. (We are so relieved the NFL finally changed the team name in 2020 so we can stop having this particular conversation.)

Meet people where they are.
Although we'd love to see it happen, white women aren't likely to move from the stages of Immersion to Balance overnight. When we meet people where they are, we wonder, Why might they be doing/saying this? How do I see myself in them? What would they have to recognize in themselves to change? These reflections help to remind us that we are connected in this struggle, as well as providing room for everyone to grow.

The same goes for systems change. We frequently work with organizations that have brought in an awesome keynote speaker to "tell it like it is" and then end up spending months or years dealing with backlash, rather than moving forward. Although we feel the urgency for change, we know that a well-thought-out strategic approach moves organizations quicker. Sometimes this means starting the conversation with "diversity" versus "white supremacist culture."

Now, if we don't ever graduate from kindergarten in the change work, that's another kind of issue to address. *Overusing* the approach of "meeting people where they are" to rationalize why progress can't take place in an organization is a form of resistance. This may have more to do with maintaining hegemony than with using this strategy.

Work collectively to end oppression.
Rugged individualism will not result in a more collaborative society. There are many times where we have acted alone, often due to a perceived sense of urgency, and later realized we made the situation worse. Working alone also gives us the sense that we are smarter than other white anti-racists or even People of Color, which rarely ends up being true or ending well.

Part of the value in working together is that we have other people with whom we are in a relationship (we love our accountabilibuddies). They can encourage us to show up and keep coming back, especially when it is hard. Working across generations can help us learn from those who have been trying to figure out this mess for a long time and those who bring a fresh perspective.

As one workshop participant put it, "I will seek to find myself in (1) caucus groups, (2) places to listen and follow the lead of People of Color, and (3) diverse groups of people."

There are several national organizing efforts we can connect with, including Showing Up for Racial Justice (ShowingUpFor RacialJustice.org) and The People's Institute for Survival and Beyond. We can also organize book groups or other small group discussions and actions. Tilman and Ilsa can't overstate how much we need each other.

Connect with People of Color

Give relationships with People of Color time to develop.
Although relationships across our differences won't end structural oppression, our deepest growth in understanding white privilege has come as a result of our friendships with People of Color. If your social circle is all or mostly white, find opportunities to be in community with People of Color activists.

At the same time, many have noted and even joked about white people's tendency to overstate the closeness of our relationships with a Person of Color. We may claim to have friends we never actually spend time with, many times using this "friend" to prove we are not racist.

For good reason, People of Color often mistrust white people in first meeting us. Get to know People of Color and give time for trust to develop instead of expecting intimacy right away. Don't take it personally if a Person of Color doesn't immediately assume you're as nice as you think you are, even if you are attending a racial justice event.

Listen carefully, believe, and check understanding.
Ijeoma Oluo shared this tip regarding how to receive feedback:

> If someone confronts you with your privilege from a place
> of anger or even hatred, if someone does not want to take
> the time or does not have the emotional energy to further
> explain to you where your privilege lies, know that it is still
> a kindness. Try to remember that the alternative to not
> being made aware of your privilege (no matter what the
> sting) is your continued participation in the oppression of
> others. Someone is giving you an opportunity to do better,
> no matter how unpleasant the delivery. Thank them.[9]

When People of Color share their experiences with racism, believe them. Especially if their experience was with you.

Anyone who has ever received the gift of deep listening knows
how good it can feel to be heard. In cross-cultural relationships,
often what we think we hear is not what is being said. Take a
moment to repeat words back to check for understanding in a
dialogue. Some helpful prompts include, "I heard...I saw...May
I reflect back for clarity? I think I heard...Will you say more
about...?"

Most women can relate to a man trying to solve our problem
for us when what we wanted was to vent or process verbally. We're
perfectly capable of figuring out our own solution, thank you very
much. Yet we may do the same to People of Color, thinking about
how we would respond in a situation, rather than genuinely listening. If a Person of Color shares an experience of racism with
you, be prepared to listen for as long as needed without interrupting, trying to offer a fix, or even offering an opinion. Ask if
they are looking for you to do something. Remember, listening is
a form of action.

Try to hold multiple truths at the same time. Given our pro-
pensity to see our experiences as the norm, white people have to
remind ourselves we have a particular racialized lens, not THE
TRUTH. Actively seek out different narratives to stories you hear

in the news and life so you are better prepared to believe someone whose experience doesn't reflect the dominant narrative.

Circle back and apologize.
As discussed in Balance, circling back means erring on the side of making amends for harm caused, even if the other person didn't feel like it was harmful or you fear reopening wounds. This is done in a spirit of truth and reconciliation, rather than an apology to make us feel better. Years after we committed a racist action, the authors have both sent letters and emails to people acknowledging what we did, what we learned, and offering an apology. Sometimes we hear back; sometimes we don't; sometimes the person doesn't even know what we're talking about. But it has never made the relationship worse.

Follow the lead of People of Color to change racist systems.
Most of the strategies in this chapter focus on the interpersonal. These interpersonal skill sets will help us better advocate for changing laws, policies, and institutions. As discussed in the Balance chapter, there are many more ways to take action and advocate than we can capture in a few pages. Instead, we encourage you to identify an area of your interest and your circle of influence, and then follow the lead of those most marginalized. Communities of Color could use more white people practicing good followership in advocating against racism.

Final Thoughts (For Now)
It is always difficult to know where to end a piece of writing. Just as we finish, another racist event will gain national attention, or a personal experience will provide more examples and insights we want to share. With that said, we hope that you use this book as a guide, that you will find yourself in a difficult situation and remember to return to a section for support and reflection. We imagine this book serving as a tool to help you cross the canyon and stay in better alignment with values of radical love and justice.

Just because we "get it" theoretically doesn't mean we've changed our behaviors for good. We do not wake up in the morning and actively prepare to feel superior to People of Color, to minimize their experiences and ideas, to aim microaggressions at them, and to boost our self-esteem by cutting them down. But this occurs. Frequently. Even with us trying to prevent it from occurring. Even when we study and teach how to NOT do this—we do it. This is important for us to recognize because it is in this humility that we can support one another as white women, being honest in our critiques while deeply connecting with, and seeing ourselves in, one another.

Community Conversations: A Guide for Collective Praxis

The right acknowledgment of Black justice, humanity,
freedom and happiness won't be found in your book clubs,
protest signs, chalk talks or organizational statements.
It will be found in your earnest willingness to dismantle
systems that stand in our way—be they at your job, in your
social network, your neighborhood associations, your family
or your home. It's not just about amplifying our voices,
it's about investing in them and in our businesses, education,
political representation, power, housing and art.
It starts, also, with reflection on the harm you've
probably caused in a Black person's life.

— Tre Johnson

Getting it Together

We intentionally co-authored this book to counter the narrative
of white women needing to compete rather than collaborate with
one another. Much of the content came from workshops where
we engaged with other white women on a journey of personal
growth and collective action. We recognize the necessity of learning together to better address racism in our own lives, workplaces,
and communities and to challenge one another to be honest about
the harm we've caused to Black, Indigenous, and other People of
Color. Although charismatic leaders get a lot of press, no social

movement happens through the work of solo individuals. In that spirit, we offer this guide for community conversations, in the hopes that you can create a group of "accountabilibuddies" who critique, support, and encourage one another to take this text beyond the pages.

You may be thinking, "But I'm not an organizer. Where do I even start?" It might be easiest to start by inviting three friends to join you in conversations and grow from there. If you are in a workplace with affinity groups or employee resource groups, you could read and practice these exercises together.

As you form your group, discuss and name your collective goals up front. In what ways do you hope discussing your experiences relative to the model in the book will help you in your growth toward Balance and Integration? In what ways will your time together help to drive change for social justice in your community? As Tre Johnson's quote above clearly states, just another book club for white people won't alleviate racism.

Although our primary intended audience is groups of white women, and we believe white caucuses are an important space for social justice work, you may also find it informative to have cross-race dialogues about *What's Up with White Women*? If you choose to gather with only white people to reflect on the text, make sure you have a way to share out publicly and/or with Black, Indigenous, and other People of Color in your lives who are interested in your progress. This work should never be done in secret or without the intention of making changes that People of Color can see or feel. A helpful rule when you do share back is "What's said here stays here. What's learned here leaves here."

Things to Consider: Some Unhelpful Common Patterns of White Women

Over many years, when we gather with white women, we've observed several patterns of engaging with one another that can reinforce internalized sexism and white superiority and hinder our growth. We offer the following checklist to help you to identify these behaviors in yourself and name them as they come up in your group.

Check which of the following things you have said or done in race conversations with white women.

☐ Believing I'm the exception.

    ☐ Talking about other white people, perhaps in other communities, who are the "real problem."

    ☐ Asking how we get people to show up to this group who don't understand the issues like we do.

Instead try recognizing there is no such thing as "getting it" when it comes to addressing racism and that we all have work to do. Celebrate the people who choose to show up and strategize about who you will share your learning with outside of this group.

☐ Competing with other white people.

    ☐ Sharing how much I know rather than how much I'm learning.

    ☐ Competing with other white women to demonstrate how committed I am to anti-racism.

    ☐ Coming from a place of righteousness in showing other white people the truth about racism.

    ☐ Quickly judging a person's intellect based on how they are dressed.

    ☐ Listening more closely to white men and/or interrupting white women more frequently than men.

    ☐ Believing there is nothing other white people can teach me about racism and wondering how we're supposed to address the topic without a Person of Color there to guide us.

Instead try sharing new insights about yourself, how you've colluded with institutional racism, and your plans to do differently. Actively listen to the reflections of others, and share what you relate to in their stories. (Avoid saying, "I relate to what you said, but…") Noticing and becoming curious about your own biases about class, gender expression, etc.

☐ Staying silent.

    ☐ Not wanting to risk saying something wrong.

    ☐ Not wanting to offend a friend in the group.

    ☐ Waiting until I have all the right language.

Instead try recognizing that you may be misunderstood and trusting one another enough to take that risk. Try saying, "I'm not sure how to say this, but I want to share something I'm feeling" or "This isn't a fully formed thought…" Stay open to feedback as an opportunity for growth when you do inevitably make mistakes and reveal biases.

☐ Hiding behind professionalism and "niceness."
    ☐ Being "nice" by not challenging something I disagree with.
    ☐ Using questions rather than statements to assert my opinion.
    ☐ For example, "Are you sure that was what he meant?" after someone shares an experience of sexism.
    ☐ Saying, "I'm just playing Devil's advocate."

Instead try asking a genuine question about someone's perspective, such as, "Can you help me understand more about how you came to see it that way?" Own your opinions and share your viewpoint, for example, "I see it differently based on (my experience, reading, conversations, etc.)" Listen and believe that people's perceptions are their reality, rather than reinterpreting their experiences through your lens. You might ask, What stage in the model of development are we each coming from as we see the same situation from a different perspective?"

☐ Prioritizing comfort over growth.
    ☐ Smiling or laughing when I'm talking about something painful to make others feel more comfortable.
    ☐ Trying to make myself more comfortable by attempting to soothe someone else's pain.
    ☐ Saying, "It's okay."
    ☐ Patting or rubbing someone's back when they didn't explicitly invite touch.
    ☐ Telling someone to calm down.
    ☐ Reassuring the person by pointing out how much has changed or how far we've come.
    ☐ Telling another white person why what they identified as their racist behavior wasn't really that bad.

Instead try getting more comfortable with the discomfort these conversations bring up. Try to identify why you are feeling uncomfortable, especially when someone else is reflecting on their experiences. Recognize, name, and challenge the ways you've been socialized to cover up your own emotions or take care of other people in ways that minimize feelings. Empathize rather than sympathize.

Let's Get Real: Using Serial Testimony for Deep Reflection

The format for discussion we're inviting groups to try, Serial Testimony, is very structured and requires little facilitation aside from reminding one another to follow that structure. Victor Lee Lewis and Peggy McIntosh first developed this tool in 2000, and the practice has been used widely by the National SEED (Seeking Educational Equity and Diversity) Project on Inclusive Curriculum of Wellesley Centers for Women.

Serial Testimony, described by Peggy McIntosh as "the autocratic administration of time in service to the democratic distribution of time," is a time management tool that encourages each participant to voice their insights and experiences without commenting on the input of other members, including head nodding in agreement. Who gets to speak, gets listened to, gets seen as an expert, and other dynamics of power frequently show up in conversations based on our race, class, gender, other social identities, as well as our position in an organization's hierarchy. This tool counters these dynamics by giving equal time and value to each person's reflections. This approach is meant to discourage consensus building around "popular" ideas, and to elicit critical thinking grounded in our unique (but often similar) experience. Because each person has only one or two minutes to share, this process provides an efficient way for all voices to be heard in a limited amount of time.

Before using Serial Testimony, participants may resist the structure. It can feel uncomfortable and awkward in the beginning. Afterward, participants often comment on the relief they feel in being able to listen to one another without needing to respond in any way. We don't have to have words of comfort or try to figure out the "right" thing to say in response to a personal story. If someone shares an idea we don't agree with, we don't have to tell them why their idea won't work for us. We also feel the power of having someone silently witness our stories and experiences. Being truly listened to is a rare gift. Sharing and listening builds community among participants in a way debate and conversation cannot.

The Basics

1. Sit in a circle with no table or other barrier between you.
2. Choose a volunteer to be the timekeeper. Someone else keeps time when the timer speaks.
3. Share the prompt or question and then Stop, Take a Breath (STAB) together. You may want to give everyone 30 seconds to silently reflect so people aren't planning their responses as they are listening to others.
4. Whoever is ready to begin can share first and then proceed around the circle to the right.
5. Everyone has one or two minutes to respond to a prompt or question. When the time is up, the timekeeper thanks them and indicates it is time for the next person, interrupting even if they are in the middle of a sentence.
6. If someone doesn't have anything to share when it comes to them, they can pass. Circle back to them after everyone else has shared to see if they've thought of something to say later or would still like to pass.
7. As people share, try to listen in stillness. Avoid showing agreement or disagreement through words, sounds, or body language. This includes avoiding head nodding, laughing along, gasping, and other subtle cues that may elevate one person above another in the group.
8. You may want to do more than one round using the same prompt. This can lead to deeper reflection.
9. After everyone has shared, take another breath. Have people silently notice what came up in their bodies as they shared and listened. This may be a good time for quiet journaling.

10. Avoid any conversation to debrief, as this would run counter to the intention of the model. If you have several small groups doing Serial Testimony separately in the same room, don't ask anyone to report back what was said.

Reflection Topics—Examples

We use Serial Testimony in different ways and offer the following for processing this book and supporting one another in reflective actions.

1. Reflecting on Internalized Sexism and White Privilege: Hurt People Hurt People
   a. A facilitator poses one question at a time. Pause and breathe between each round. The facilitator may or may not respond to prompts and should determine power differentials within the group when deciding. Either way, make sure the group knows the facilitator's role.
   b. Participants talk about each prompt in present tense, as if it is happening right now. The facilitator interrupts briefly as necessary to remind people to speak in present tense. For example, "Say *I am*, rather than *I was*," or simply, "Present tense."
   c. As people share, they have one or two minutes to name (1) where they are, (2) who else is with them, (3) what is happening, and (4) how they are feeling. It is useful to post these four topics as a visual reminder. We've found facilitators most often need to remind people to say how they are feeling.
   d. Prompts
   Round 1: Talk about a time when you felt hurt by sexism using the present tense.
   Round 2: Talk about a time when you hurt someone because of your internalized sexism.
   Round 3: Talk about a time when you hurt someone with your white privilege.
   Round 4: Talk about a time when you felt pain because of white privilege.

2. Applying the Text to Your Life
   a. After reading a section of the book, do one or more rounds of Serial Testimony on a single prompt that connects to that section.
   b. Prompt Examples
   Talk about a time when you noticed yourself in the Buffer Zone.
   Talk about a time when you recognized you were in Immersion. Repeat this after reading about each stage of identity development.
   Talk about a time when you cried in a mixed-race group, or talk about a time when you witnessed a white woman crying in a mixed-race group.
   c. As above, share your stories in present tense and identify where, who, what, and how you're feeling.

3. Applying your Life to the Text
   a. Think about a situation where you noticed the intersection of sexism and white privilege in your life, even if you didn't identify it as such. This may be a time where you got feedback about harm you caused, a time when you had a conversation about racism, a time when you stayed silent in the face of injustice, or another instance. Try to remember a time where you felt tension.
   b. Prompts
   Round 1: Describe the situation in present tense, including where you are, who else is there, what is happening, and how you are feeling.
   Round 2: Talk more about how you are feeling and why.
   Round 3: What stage of the model were you in? What are the indicators of that stage? Alternatively, how do you see this connected to the intersection of sexism and white privilege?
   Round 4: What, if anything, would you do differently if you could?

4. Case Studies

This is a slightly different way of using Serial Testimony. A single case study will be presented, and everyone in the group will respond with their best thinking about what to do in this situation. Case studies from current events or stories from the book can be used as well.

Case studies help participants think more about creative action steps. Even if an individual has never experienced the circumstances being discussed, they can often generalize the ideas shared to other situations in their life.

a. The presenter succinctly describes the issues, being clear as to what they need support around. They pose a question to the group (five to ten minutes).

b. Participants may then ask clarifying questions (three to five minutes). A clarifying question gives more information needed to respond thoughtfully, such as, "What was the race and gender of everyone involved?" This is different from a leading question, such as, "Have you tried...?"

c. Identify a recorder, someone who is not presenting the case study, to take notes. These notes are given to the presenter at the end of the session so they can listen attentively to each speaker. Someone else takes notes when the recorder speaks.

d. Every participant is encouraged to give feedback, regardless of their experience (one or two minutes each). Feedback may be in the form of questions, critique, a personal story, a suggestion, etc., focused on speaking from your unique experience. This is not a time to try to shame the presenter; nor is it a time to reassure them they don't have anything to work on.

e. The presenter does not respond as people share, even if they ask a question. Those questions will be recorded in the notes for the presenter to reflect on later.

f. After the first round, you may go around again, the presenter may ask a second question of the whole group (not in response to something someone said), or you may stop.

g. When finished, the person presenting the case study may thank the group but does not respond to anyone. Avoid the urge to speak to what you've already tried or what you found particularly useful.

Focus Group Participants

*One of the most powerful social and political catalysts of the past
has been the speaking of women with other women, the telling of
our secrets, the comparing of wounds, and the sharing of words.*

— Adrienne Rich

The Seattle focus group included the following people:

CHRIS SCHAFER is in her mid-thirties and has spent a substantial amount of time living abroad as an adult.

JOHANNA EAGER is a cisgender, queer white woman in her early fifties. She grew up in a small rural town in southern Minnesota where it wasn't safe to come out. This experience helped her to develop empathy for anyone suffering the pain of oppression. She's spent decades working on understanding her privileged identities, in particular, her whiteness, for the purpose of dismantling white supremacy and seeking racial justice. Johanna is a national diversity, equity, and inclusion leader with her own consulting practice. Due to being diagnosed with breast cancer, she was not able to participate in all the focus groups.

KATY GREENLEAF is a straight, cisgender woman in her mid forties who grew up in a middle-class family in a suburb an hour outside of Seattle, Washington. Situated near two military bases, it was an ethnically and socioeconomically diverse area. When she moved to Seattle to attend UW, she was confused by the lack of diversity in her classes and segregation throughout the city.

Now her work as a feminist therapist incorporates information about how systemic racism, sexism, and heterosexism contribute to mental health challenges. She is also the mother of two cisgender, white children, and works to increase their awareness of their many privileges, while balancing that with compassion for the shared human experience.

MALLORY CLARKE, a straight, cisgender woman, grew up in several cities on the west coast and spent four formative years in New Orleans during the Civil Rights Movement. Now in her sixties and retired from teaching struggling teenagers to read, she spends time as a wildlife tracker, an activist, a writer, and a budding naturalist. She treasures connection with her daughter and an adopted grandson.

TERRIE YAFFE is a cisgender woman born into a Jewish family and community in the 1950s near Asbury Park, NJ. She moved to Pacific NW in the '70s and raised her child. As a mother and as an advocate and educator for children experiencing all kinds of losses and childhood disruptions due to family homelessness and domestic violence, she's committed herself to doing the emotional labor required to confront and understand her experience of white privilege, past and present, and to acknowledge how she benefits. To stay embodied and present and move through her discomfort toward social action, Terrie depends on some physical practices that include meditation and dance.

The groups at the White Privilege Conference included the following people:

BETH APPLEGATE is a cisgender lesbian woman in her late fifties, and happily partnered for over twenty years. Beth is currently an organization development (OD) practitioner-scholar and a racial justice educator, author, and speaker. Beth was born and raised in Bloomington, Indiana, then lived in the DC metro area for over two decades before returning to Btown to care for her parents. She is a certified Brené Brown Dare to Lead™ facilitator, a member of the Catalyst-Ed's diversity, equity and inclusion (DEI) national team, and the former national Field Director for National Abortion and Reproductive Rights Action League (NARAL).

BETH YOHE is a cisgender, straight, middle-class, happily married parent in her forties. She was born in Iowa, grew up in Texas, and has made her home in Colorado. She is the Executive Director of a small nonprofit in Denver and will always be a facilitator at heart.

CHRISTINE SAXMAN is the founder of Saxman Consulting LLC, where she provides racial and social justice training, facilitation, and coaching. She also works each summer for the National SEED Project (Seeking Education Equity and Diversity) as part of the national staff. Prior to spending two years as an equity transformation specialist at Courageous Conversations About Race, Christine was an educator in Township District 113 in Illinois for fifteen years, where she was also a racial equity leader. In 2016, she received recognition as an Illinois Golden Apple Finalist and Teacher of Distinction. She earned a BA in English from University of Pittsburgh, an MA in English from Northwestern University, and an MS in Education from Northwestern University. She can be found at christinesaxman.com.

DENA SAMUELS, PHD, was born in South Africa, moved to the US and grew up on the east coast. She is a cisgender, bisexual woman who has lived in Colorado for 25 years—which is just shy of half her life. She recently left a tenured faculty position at a university to consult full time as a mindfulness-based diversity, equity, and inclusion catalyst.

ILANA MARCUCCI-MORRIS is a thirty-four-year-old California Queer Momma. She's a cisgender, clinical social worker and cabaret ActivARTist building Revolutionary anti-racist community through relationship-building, family-making, the stage, and public service. She is married to an amazing woman and mom, a fellow trauma steward, and they're raising their son to be conscious of his whiteness and leverage subsequent privileges to combat all forms of oppression.

LAURA REMINGTON MOORE is a white, straight, cisgender woman who grew up in the Midwest and spent time in Seattle and New York City. She holds a bachelor's degree in special education from the University Wisconsin Oshkosh and a master's degree in higher education administration from the University of Kansas. She has taught adjunct classes at the college level on white privilege and done presentations on white privilege and raising Black children. She currently lives in Green Bay with her husband and their two children. For the past ten years, she's raised their children while volunteering in her community around education issues, the White Privilege Conference, and African Heritage Inc.

DR. PEGGY MCINTOSH is a white cisgender heterosexual woman living in Massachusetts with her best friend Ken McIntosh, who has been involved with coronaviruses ever since he discovered the third one known to humans in 1967. Many kinds of injustice join our work in this pandemic year of 2020.

ROBIN DIANGELO, PHD, grew up in poverty in the Bay Area and was raised white, female, and Catholic. Her experience of sexism and classism have been powerful entry points to understanding her internalization of white supremacy. She is in her sixties, a former professor who now writes and speaks on racism and white racial identity. She is the author of many publications and books on whiteness, including *White Fragility: Why It's So Hard For White People To Talk About Racism*.

SHELLY TOCHLUK is a straight woman who grew up in Orange County, California, in a middle-class home with two parents. She moved to Los Angeles and became racially aware while teaching elementary school in Inglewood, California. Shelly now teaches teachers as a professor at a small liberal arts college. She is the author of *Witnessing Whiteness* and a supporter of white people in their racial identity development. She is a proud dog mom.

There was one phone interview participant:

JESSICA PETTITT is a native Texan who has lived all over the country, largely due to being fired a lot. She's in her late forties, a white, cisgender woman. She's lesbian identified, happily married to a transman, and co-parent of three large mutts. She's working as a professional speaker and author at GoodEnoughNow.com.

Definitions

In our workshops, we ask people to read these definitions and reflect on how they respond to them. This gives us a common foundation to enter deeper conversations.

Cisgender (or Cis): A term that describes a person whose gender identity aligns with the sex assigned to them at birth.

Gender: A person's internal sense of self as male, female, both, or neither (gender identity), as well as one's outward presentation and behaviors (gender expression). Gender norms vary among cultures and over time.

Gender identity: An internal, deeply felt sense of being male, female, a blend of both, or neither—how individuals perceive themselves and what they call themselves. One's gender identity can be the same or different from their sex assigned at birth.

Internalized Oppression: When members of a target group believe, act on, or enforce the dominant system of beliefs about themselves and members of their own group. For example, **internalized sexism** involves women applying principals of male dominance and oppression to themselves and/or other women.

Internalized Superiority: When members of an agent group accept their group's socially and politically superior status as normal and deserved. For example, **internalized white superiority** is the belief and actions based on the idea that white people are superior.

Intersectionality: An approach largely advanced by Women of Color, arguing that classifications such as gender, race, class, and others cannot be examined in isolation from one another; they interact and intersect in individuals' lives, in society, in social systems, and are mutually constitutive.

Microaggressions: A statement, action, or incident regarded as an instance of indirect, subtle, or unintentional discrimination against members of a marginalized group.

Oppression: Systemic devaluing, undermining, marginalizing, and disadvantaging of certain social identities in contrast to the privileged norm; when some people are denied something of value, while others have ready access.

Privilege: Systemic favoring, enriching, valuing, validating, and including of certain social identities over others. Individuals cannot "opt out" of systems of privilege; rather these systems are inherent to the society in which we live.

Race: There is no biological basis for racial categories, and genetic research has shown we have more within-group variations than between-group variations. Races are socially and politically constructed categories assigned based on physical characteristics, such as skin color or hair type. Although there are no races, perceptions of race influence our beliefs and stereotypes, economic opportunities, and everyday experiences.

Racism: Institutional power + prejudice against subordinated members of targeted racial groups (Blacks, Latinx, Native Americans, Asians) by members of the agent racial group (whites). This happens at the individual, cultural, and institutional levels. Racism can involve both conscious action and unconscious collusion. In other words, it need not be intentional.

Sexism: A system of oppression that privileges men, subordinates women, and denigrates women-identified values. This subordination occurs at the individual, cultural, and institutional levels.

White Privilege: A system of unearned benefits afforded to people classified as white. These advantages are personal, cultural, and institutional and provide greater access to resources and systemic power. For white people, white privilege leads to a form of oppression as it distorts their relationships and humanity.

White Supremacy: The assumption or theory that whites are superior to all other races and should be in power and control.

Definitions adapted from the following sources:

2014 White Privilege Conference: Whiteprivilegeconference.com

The People's Institute of Survival and Beyond: pisab.org/

Welcoming Schools: welcomingschools.org/resources/definitions
/definitions-for-adults/

Wijeysinghe, C. L., Griffin, P., and Love, B. "Racism Curriculum Design." In Chris Adams, L. A. Bell, & P. Griffin (Eds.), *Teaching for Diversity and Social Justice: A Sourcebook* (pp. 82–109). New York: Routledge, 1997.

Focus Group Participant Book List

DiAngelo, O. S. *Is Everyone Really Equal? An Introduction to Key Concepts in Social Justice Education.* New York: Teachers College Press, 2017.

DiAngelo, R. *What Does It Mean to Be White? Developing White Racial Literacy.* New York: Peter Lang Publishing, Inc., 2016.

DiAngelo, R. *White Fragility: Why It's So Hard for White People to Talk about Racism.* Boston: Beacon Press, 2018.

McIntosh, P. *On Privilege, Fraudulence, and Teaching as Learning.* New York: Routledge, 2020.

Pettitt, J. *Good Enough Now: How Doing the Best We Can with What We Have is Better than Nothing.* Shippensburg: Sound Wisdom, 2017.

Samuels, D. *The Culturally Inclusive Educator.* New York: Teachers College, 2014.

Samuels, D. *The Mindfulness Effect: An Unexpected Path to Healing, Connection, & Social Justice.* Denver: Night River Press, 2018.

Tochluk, S. *Witnessing Whiteness: The Need to Talk about Race and How to Do It.* Lanham: Rowman & Littlefield Education, 2010.

Tochluk, S. *Living in the Tension: The Quest for a Spiritualized Racial Justice.* Roselle: Crandall, Dostie, & Douglass Books, Inc, 2016.

Notes

Chapter 2: A Power Analysis: White Women and Institutional Access

1. D. J. DeGruy, *Be the Healing* (Town Hall, Seattle, Washington, United States, April 4, 2019).
2. S. E. James, *The Report of the 2015 U.S. Transgender Survey* (Washington, DC: National Center for Transgender Equality, 2015).
3. Peoples Institute, *Definitions* (New Orleans, Louisiana, n.d.).
4. I. A. Siegelman, "Race and Gender Discrimination in Bargaining for a New Car," *The American Economic Review* (1995).
5. S. Mullainathan, "Racial Bias, Even When We Have Good Intentions," *New York Times Economic Review*, n.d.
6. D. Kandiyoti, "Bargaining with Patriarchy," *Gender and Society*, no. 23, (September 1988): 274–290.
7. J. Phlegar, "The Reality of Patriarchal Bargain," Feministing June 15, 2015, www.feministing.com
8. P. Kivel, *Uprooting Racism: How White People Can Work for Racial Justice* (Gabriola Island: New Society Publishers, 2017).
9. M. M. Ngai, "From Colonial Subject to Undesirable Alien: Filipino Migration in the Invisible Empire," in *Impossible Subjects: Illegal Aliens and the Making of Modern America* (Princeton: Princeton University Press, 2004), 116.
10. M. M. Accapadi, "When White Women Cry: How White Women's Tears Oppress Women of Color," *The College Student Affairs Journal*, (Spring 2007).

Chapter 3: A Model of White Women's Development

1. A. Darder, *Culture and Power in the Classroom: Educational Foundations for the Schooling of Bicultural Students* (Boulder: Paradigm Publishers, 2012).
2. J. Loewen, *Sundown Towns: A Hidden Dimension of American Racism.* New York: The New Press, 2005).

3. R. Menakem, *My Grandmother's Hands: Racialized Trauma and the Pathway to Mending Our Hearts and Bodies*. Las Vegas: Central Recovery Press, 2017).

4. F. P. Hutchinson, (1997). "Strategic Questioning: An Approach to Creating Personal and Social Change," *Active Democracy*, (1997): 1–24.

Chapter 4: Immersion

1. M. V. Harris-Perry, *Sister Citizen: Shame, Stereotypes, and Black Women in America* (New Haven & London: Yale University Press, 2011), 18.

2. B. Roe and P. Jumper Thurman, "Violence against native women," *Social Justice* 31(2004): 70–86.

3. S. Truth, *Ain't I a Woman!* In I. Linwaite, *Ain't I a Woman! Classic Poetry by Women from Around the World* (Lincolnwood, Illinois, United States: Contemporary Books, 2000), 182.

4. K. Manne, "Brett Kavanaugh and America's 'Himpathy' Reckoning," *The New York Times*, September 26, 2018.

5. K. Blaine, (2016, January 19). Buzz Feed News. Retrieved from Buzz Feed News: buzzfeednews.com/article/kyleblaine/so-uh-heres-the -full-text-of-sarah-palins-bizarre-trump-spee

6. P. Williams, (2018, September 17). New Yorker Magazine. Retrieved from New Yorker Magazine: newyorker.com/magazine/2018/09/24 /sarah-huckabee-sanders-trumps-battering-ram

7. A. Lorde, *Sister Outsider: Essays and Speeches by Audre Lorde*. Berkeley: Crossing Press, 1984, 2007), 47–48.

8. M. V. Harris-Perry, *Sister Citizen: Shame, Stereotypes, and Black Women in America*. New Haven & London: Yale University Press, 2011), 29.

9. L. L. Dorr, *White Women, Rape, and the Power of Race in Virginia 1900–1960* (Chapel Hill and London: The University of North Carolina Press, 2004), 7–8.

10. I. B. Wells, *Southern Horrors: Lynch Law in All Its Phases* (Auckland: The Floating Press, 2014) 11–12.

11. J. Bouie, "The Deadly History of 'They're Raping Our Women,'" Slate, June 18, 2015, slate.com/articles/news_and_politics/history/2015/06 /the_deadly_history_of_they_re_raping_our_women_racists_have _long_defended.html

Chapter 5: Capitulation

1. Belenky et al., *Women's Ways of Knowing: The Development of Self, Voice, and Mind*. New York: BasicBooks, 2007).

2. U. D. Rights, *Civil Rights Data Collection: Data Snapshot (School Discipline)* (2014, March 21).

3. P. H. Collins, *Toward a New Vision: Race, Class, and Gender as Categories of Analysis and Connection*. In *Race, Class, and Gender*, 1993, 650.

Chapter 6: Defense

1. G. Steinem, *My Life on the Road* (New York: Random House, 2015), 165.

2. Steinem. *My Life on the Road*, 167–170.

3. A. Y. Davis, *Women Race & Class* (New York: Vintage Books, 1983), 38–39.

4. Davis. *Women Race & Class*, 40.

5. Davis. *Women Race & Class*, 44.

6. Davis. *Women Race & Class*, 51.

7. Davis. *Women Race & Class*, 51–59.

8. nativeappropriations.com/2010/04/but-why-cant-i-wear-a-hipster-headdress.html

9. A. Garza, *The Purpose of Power: How we Come Together when we Fall Apart.* (New York: One World, 2020), 34.

10. J. Landsman, "The State of the White Woman Teacher," in *The Guide for White Women Who Teach Black Boys*, ed. A. M.-P. Eddie Moore (Thousand Oaks: Corwin, 2018), 28–39.

11. S. Morrison, "Ani DiFranco Cancelled Her 'Righteous Retreat' to a Former Slave Plantation," *The Atlantic*, December 29, 2013.

12. J. B. NoiseCat, "His side of the story: Nathan Phillips wants to talk about Covington," *The Guardian*, February 4, 2019, theguardian.com/us-news/2019/feb/04/nathan-phillips-his-story-hate-division-covington

Chapter 7: Projection

1. J. L. Calderón, *Occupying Privilege: Conversations on Love, Race and Liberation* (Love-N-Liberation Liberation Press, 2012), 43.

Chapter 8: Balance

1. M. Segrest, *Memoir of a Race Traitor* (Boston: South End Press, 1994), 168.

2. P. Freire, *Pedagogy of the Oppressed* (New York: Continuum, 1986).

3. L. Nieto and M. Boyer, *Beyond Inclusion, Beyond Empowerment.* (Olympia: Cuetzpalin, 2010).

4. K. Crenshaw, "Kimberlé Crenshaw—On Intersectionality—keynote—WOW 2016: Southbank Centre," *Southbank Centre at YouTube*, May 18, 2018.

5. D. Sue and D. Sue, *Counseling the Culturally Diverse: Theory and Practice* (New York: John Wiley, 2003), 18.

6. M. E. Dyson, *Tears We Cannot Stop: A Sermon to White America* (New York: St. Martin's Press, 2017), 216.

7. S. E. Cronin. *Soy Bilingüe: Adult Dual Language Model for Early Childhood and Elementary Teacher Education.* Seattle: Center for Linguistic and Cultural Democracy, 2008), 170–175.

8. J. Loewen, *Lies Across America: What Our Historic Sites Get Wrong* (New York: The New Press, 1999), 84–88.

9. Sue. *Counseling the Culturally Diverse: Theory and Practice*, 150.

10. R. Frankenberg, *The Social Construction of Whiteness: White Women, Race Matters* (Minneapolis: University of Minnesota Press, 1993), 6.

11. E. Goldman, *Living My Life.* (New York: Cosimo Classics, 1931).

Chapter 9: Integration

1. V. Kaur, *Three Lessons of Revolutionary Love*, November 2017, Retrieved from TED: ted.com/talks/valarie_kaur_3_lessons_of _revolutionary_love_in_a_time_of_rage?language=en

2. S. Butler and R. Butler, (directors). *Mirrors of Privilege: Making Whiteness Visible,"* motion picture, 2006.

3. D. T. Dalai Lama. *The Book of Joy* (New York: Avery, 2016), 201.

Chapter 10: White Women's Tears

1. A. G. Morales, interviewed by I. Govan, March 2018.

2. C. D. Hollins, interviewed by I. Govan, March 2018.

3. R. DiAngelo and Ö. Sensoy, (2012). "Getting Slammed: White Depictions of Race Discussions as Arenas of Violence." *Race Ethnicity and Education* (2012), DOI:10.1080/13613324.2012.674023.

4. J. Loubriel, "4 Ways White People Can Process Their Emotions Without Bringing the White Tears," *Everyday Feminism* (February 16, 2016).

5. M. M. Accapadi, "When White Women Cry: How White Women's Tears Oppress Women of Color," *The College Student Affairs Journal* (Spring 2007): 209.

6. Eddie Moore, Jr., *The Guide for White Women Who Teach Black Boys* (2018, January 17).

7. M. Tauber, "Paula Deen 'I'm Fighting to Get My Name Back,'" *People*, March 10, 2014.

8. I. Shapira, "The Daily Show springs tense showdown with Native Americans on Redskins fans." *The Washington Post*, September 19, 2014.

9. M. Segrest, *Born to Belonging: Writings on Spirit and Justice* (New Brunswick, New Jersey, and London: Rutgers University Press, 2002), 165.

Chapter 11: If What, Now What?

1. M. R. Castaneda, *Cultural Democracy, Bicognitive Development, and Education* (New York: Academic Press, Inc., 1974).

2. R. Kegan and L. Laskow Lahey, *Immunity to Change: How to Overcome it and Unlock Potential in Yourself and Your Organization*. Boston: Harvard Business Press, 2009).

3. R. Charles, *Rupaul's Drag Race*, Logo TV, 2009–2018.

4. Obear, 2017.

5. M. R. Banaji and A. G. Greenwald, *Blindspot: Hidden Biases of Good People* (New York: Delacorte Press, 2013).

6. T. Okun, (2000). "dRworks," Dismantling Racism Works, 2000, dismantlingracism.org/

7. A. Boal, *Theater of the Oppressed*. (London: Pluto Press, 1979).

8. M. Rosenberg, *Nonviolent Communication: A Language of Life* (Encinitas: Puddle Dancer Press, 2005).

9. I. Oluo, *So You Want to Talk about Race* (New York: Seal Press, 2018), 68.

Index

About the Authors

TILMAN SMITH has been an educator, project manager, and racial justice consultant for over thirty-five years, serving as a classroom teacher, college instructor, caucus facilitator, trainer, and coach. She has facilitated workshops and caucuses throughout the country on the topics of racial equity, white privilege, internalized sexism, and internalized white superiority. She lives in Seattle, Washington.

ILSA GOVAN has extensive experience as an anti-racist facilitator, consultant, leadership coach, and activist. As co-founder of Cultures Connecting, she has helped countless organizations put their vision of racial equity into practice. Her facilitation superpower is guiding white people in examining how we've internalized racism in our assumptions and actions. She lives in Seattle, Washington.

Proceeds from *What's Up with White Women? Unpacking Sexism and White Privilege in Pursuit of Racial Justice* benefit Tsuru for Solidarity and The Unspoken Truths. Please join us in supporting their important work. For details, visit https://www.culturesconnecting.com/donations

ABOUT NEW SOCIETY PUBLISHERS

New Society Publishers is an activist, solutions-oriented publisher focused on publishing books to build a more just and sustainable future. Our books offer tips, tools, and insights from leading experts in a wide range of areas.

We're proud to hold to the highest environmental and social standards of any publisher in North America. When you buy New Society books, you are part of the solution!

At New Society Publishers, we care deeply about *what* we publish—but also about *how* we do business.

- All our books are printed on 100% **post-consumer recycled paper**, processed chlorine-free, with low-VOC vegetable-based inks (since 2002). We print all our books in North America (never overseas)

- Our corporate structure is an innovative employee shareholder agreement, so we're one-third employee-owned (since 2015)

- We've created a Statement of Ethics (2021). The intent of this Statement is to act as a framework to guide our actions and facilitate feedback for continuous improvement of our work

- We're carbon-neutral (since 2006)

- We're certified as a B Corporation (since 2016)

- We're Signatories to the UN's Sustainable Development Goals (SDG) Publishers Compact (2020–2030, the Decade of Action)

To download our full catalog, sign up for our quarterly newsletter, and to learn more about New Society Publishers, please visit newsociety.com

ENVIRONMENTAL BENEFITS STATEMENT

New Society Publishers saved the following resources by printing the pages of this book on chlorine free paper made with 100% post-consumer waste.

TREES	WATER	ENERGY	SOLID WASTE	GREENHOUSE GASES
43	3,400	18	140	18,500
FULLY GROWN	GALLONS	MILLION BTUs	POUNDS	POUNDS

Environmental impact estimates were made using the Environmental Paper Network Paper Calculator 4.0. For more information visit www.papercalculator.org

MIX
Paper from responsible sources
FSC® C016245